The

WEE

Christopher Somerville was brought up in Gloucestershire and educated in Dorset and Brighton and at Durham University. In 1974 he began his teaching career, but writing gradually took over. He has written a dozen books, including *Coastal Walks in England and Wales* (Grafton), *Britain beside the Sea* (Grafton) and *The Other British Isles* (Grafton). He has written numerous pieces for the *Sunday Times* Travel Section, *Sunday Telegraph Magazine* and the *Independent Sunday Review*. He has a regular 'Walk of the Month' column in the *Saturday Telegraph*. He has made many appearances on the radio, including his role as compiler/presenter of three series of 'Literary Walks' with authors for Radio 4, and presents an ongoing series of country walks on Anglia TV.

The Daily Telegraph

BOOK OF

WEEKEND WALKS

CHRISTOPHER SOMERVILLE

PAN BOOKS
LONDON, SYDNEY AND AUCKLAND

First published 1993 by Pan Books Ltd

a division of Pan Macmillan Publishers Limited
Cavaye Place London SW10 9PG
and Basingstoke

Associated companies throughout the world

ISBN 0 330 32658 9

Maps © The Daily Telegraph
Photos © Christopher Somerville except where otherwise stated

1 3 5 7 9 8 6 4 2

A CIP catalogue for this book is available from
the British Library

Photoset by Parker Typesetting Service, Leicester
Printed and bound in Great Britain by
Cox & Wyman Ltd, Reading, Berkshire

FOR JANE

One day . . .!

and for my Godfather, A. H. 'Bobby' Brewin,
with affectionate thanks for his
comments and encouragement

Contents

Introduction

When I began to write the 'Walk of the Month' features in the Travel Section of the *Weekend Telegraph* in September 1990, I had in mind two kinds of reader – those who enjoy a good step-out at the weekend and would actually want to follow the walks, and those who prefer to do their rambling in spirit from the comfort of an armchair. I'd assumed that nearly all would be armchair ramblers, and that Saturday's breakfast table reading (like most journalism) would be wrapping Sunday's fish and chips.

But *Telegraph* readers seemed to have other ideas. I began to get comments from farmers and pub landlords along the walk routes – sightings of strange individuals and small groups of adventurers, clutching flapping pages torn from a newspaper, striding the footpaths or comparing notes over their ploughman's lunches. Letters started arriving at the *Telegraph* from all over the country. Some walkers had had childhood memories stirred; some were rejoicing at having discovered a new place to explore. Some admonished me for slip-ups, others suggested improvements or alternatives to my routes.

Many wrote to complain that their sheaves of torn-out *Telegraph* pages were becoming too tattered to use. Could they please have the walks collected manageably between covers? Hence this complete collection of the first two years of *Weekend Telegraph* 'Weekend Walks', revised and corrected according to readers' suggestions.

Country walking is the most popular leisure activity in Britain today. Yet many people who might enjoy a walk are put off by the image of rambling as something that involves a backpack of paratrooper proportions and weight, clumping great boots, expert knowledge of map and compass, and much sweat and agony over thirty miles of mountain and moorland. The twenty-four walks between these covers are nothing like that. Only one is really tough – the Bangor Trail through the bleak Nephin Beg Mountains in County Mayo, Ireland. A few of the others – Glen Clova in Scotland, Upper Teesdale, the East Kielder Burn in Northumberland, the superb week-long ramble through the Cerdagne region of the French Pyrenees – are set in countryside lonely and wild enough to satisfy those who like a spice of challenge to their walking.

Most of these walks, however, are easy-paced rambles through the beautiful landscape of England, Wales and Scotland, circular walks a few miles long that anyone reasonably fit can enjoy. You don't need to be a hairy-kneed heather-basher to try out these walks; just someone who wants a bit of gentle exercise in lovely surroundings, a dash of history and a local legend or two, a decent pub somewhere along the route, and walking directions accurate enough to trust without being bossy.

The walks are sprinkled throughout the British Isles from Devon to the Scottish Highlands, from East Anglia to Wales. Walks in Ireland, Spain and France are featured for added interest. There are short strolls in historic city surroundings (York, London); walks based round literary personalities (the poet Edward Thomas in Hampshire, Henry Williamson in the *Tarka the Otter* country of North Devon, George Borrow in Wild Wales); walks through well-known landscapes such as the Black Mountains of Wales and Shropshire's Cardingmill Valley, and those in little-known but fascinating places like Nettleton Beck in Lincolnshire, and Littleton-on-Severn where the broad Severn Estuary meets the sea.

There is a strong seasonal tinge to the walks – spring among the flowers of the Burren in County Clare, Ireland; an escape from the summer crowds into the mountains behind the Costa del Sol in southern Spain; the blazing colours of the Scottish hills in autumn; a wintry walk on the Long Mynd to complement the epic survival tale of the snow-bound Revd Donald Carr.

Many of the rambles feature companions who came with me to show me the things I would certainly have missed on my own, to tell me local tall stories, to let me mine their specialized knowledge, or simply to chat away the miles. It's a pleasure to enjoy their company again in this collection: Dave Richardson of Edinburgh, musician, natural historian and nice judge of good whisky; Oliver Geraghty, young hero of the Mayo mountains; Dick Bernard with his life-long devotion to Scotland's Ochil Hills; the hospitable members of the Edward Thomas Fellowship; friends and members of my family, particularly my father, John Somerville, who has worn out plenty of shoe leather and conversation by my side over the years.

Each walk description is accompanied by a map, and by a separate section of practical information. Here you'll find details of which Ordnance Survey map to take, how to reach the start of the walk, clear walking route instructions with Ordnance Survey map reference numbers, length and approximate duration of the walk, conditions to be expected and advice on clothing and equipment, places to eat, drink and stay overnight, recommended reading and further information to help you get the very best out of your expedition.

Here are two dozen of the best walks I know. If you are encountering them for the first time, you have a treat in store. If you have already made acquaintance with them – you will be able to throw away those tattered *Telegraph* cuttings with a sigh of relief. Whether from the armchair or from the footpath, I hope you enjoy them.

CHRISTOPHER SOMERVILLE

Pilgrims' Murky Progress

THE BLACK MOUNTAINS, WELSH BORDERS

St Mary's Chapel at Capel-y-ffin, which the diarist curate Francis Kilvert
likened to 'a stout grey owl'

Turning round to admire the view from the hillside above
Capel-y-ffin, Ruth and I saw what we didn't want to see –
white shawls of cloud slipping across the Welsh border and
round the shoulders of the Vale of Ewyas. It looked as if my
daughter's fourteenth birthday was set to be a wet one. When
the Black Mountains throw this kind of a climatic tantrum, they
don't do it by halves. True to its omens, the day turned out to be
a real cloud-blanketed soaker, and we had to abandon the glorious ridge walk that I had promised Ruth. But squelching along
the narrow tracks of the Ewyas hill slopes, nibbling green hazel
nuts and blackberries from the hedges and watching buzzards
wheeling in and out of the rain curtains, the birthday girl and I
were happy enough.

I

Long ridges climbed into the sky on both sides as we drove up the twisting valley-bottom road to the start of our walk. There are remoter valleys than the Vale of Ewyas among the half-dozen that run north and west along the Welsh border towards the River Wye, but none more beautiful. The valley sweeps in a succession of grand, flowing curves up to Capel-y-ffin, where two chapels and a couple of houses cluster near the bridge over the shallow Afon Honddu.

St Mary's stands among thick-trunked, gnarled old yews, a tiny whitewashed box of a church with a crooked little bellcote on the roof. 'Like a stout grey owl,' said Francis Kilvert, the diarist curate of Clyro, when he walked over to Capel-y-ffin in September 1870. Kilvert had come to visit the Benedictine monastery being built just up the hill by the passionate holy eccentric Father Ignatius and his dedicated band of black-robed monks. It still stands there, the great church as thoroughly laid waste by a few decades of neglect as any medieval monastic ruin. In the nearby monastery building, most of it a private house these days, we found the little chapel with low rafters lettered in Latin by the sculptor Eric Gill when he lived and worked here in the 1920s.

We passed girls on horseback clopping down the monastery lane, and trudged up a stony gully on to the open hillside above Capel-y-ffin. The hooves of horses and sheep and the boots of walkers had beaten out a clear track running south-east through bracken and close-nibbled turf along the thousand-foot contour, hugging the slope under the ridge. From this narrow path we had fine views through the drifting rain, back to the bulging, cloud-shrouded shoulders at the head of the Vale of Ewyas and forward over ancient stone walls into the small hedged fields and scattered woods of the valley floor around Llanthony Priory.

Many outsiders yearning for peace both spiritual and physical have found their way into the Vale of Ewyas over the centuries, and the valley has defeated them all. Father Ignatius's Benedictine brotherhood at Capel-y-ffin lasted barely forty years, and down here at Llanthony the far statelier and more splendid buildings of the Augustinian priory housed a proper community for less than a century. Most of the original twelfth-century settlers went off to start again near Gloucester, where the climate was milder, the land less wild and the natives friendlier. Later Llanthony monks laboured over the superb rose-pink abbey church whose ruined towers, arches and pillars stand sixty feet tall on a green sward. The poet Walter Savage Landor tasted seven years of bitter fruit from the priory estate when he bought it in 1807. Landor was too lordly to get on with his rough Welsh farmer tenants, on one occasion being thrown out of an upstairs window during a quarrel over rents.

Llanthony is a more hospitable place these days. Parts of the buildings house a hotel, as they have done for two centuries. You can sleep in a four-poster in a room in one of the abbey towers, reached by a stone spiral staircase, and eat dinner in the Prior's parlour. Ruth and I, coming out of the drizzle into the darkness of the vaulted cellar bar, dripped dry over our ploughman's lunches and eavesdropped on local affairs.

Francis Kilvert visited Llanthony Abbey a couple of months before his trip to Capel-y-ffin, arriving as the Landor tenantry were assembling to pay their midsummer rents and recoup as much as they could in free food and drink laid on by their landlord. 'A savoury reek pervaded the place,' recorded Kilvert, 'and the tantalized tenants walked about lashing their tails, growling and snuffing up the scent of food hungrily like Welsh wolves.' The young curate and his brother Perch were pretty wolfish themselves after their twelve-mile walk over the hills from Clyro – they put away '18 eggs . . . and a proportionate amount of bread, cheese, butter and beer'. One suspects they had a fair wind behind them on the way back to Clyro.

After our rather less substantial meal we wandered through the arches of the abbey ruins, and then made for the track that climbs sharply uphill to the north to meet the long-distance Offa's Dyke footpath and the Welsh/English boundary on the spine of Hatterall Ridge. This long stretch of high-level striding along the gently rising ridge is one of the most exhilarating pieces of airy, windy upland walking I know. You look down on your left into the Vale of Ewyas, on your right into the sweeping and narrowing Olchon Valley which few visitors enter and fewer trouble to penetrate as far as its roadless head under the Black Hill. From the northern end of the ridge, two thousand feet in the air, the great arching foot of Hay Bluff swoops down and away into the tumbled, wrinkled country around Hay-on-Wye and the wide Wye Valley.

To follow the Hatterall Ridge on a sunny day is to mount gently into bliss. But there was no wishing away that dead grey hand of mist clamped immovably round the heights above Llanthony; nor the sluicing rain that now began to conduct an uncomfortable examination of our waterproofs. We hung around on the treeline for a few minutes, staring up grumpily into the murk, then made the best of a disappointment and found a rutted lane linking the farms on the hillside.

Massively built stone barns stood in the farmyards and fields, tiny triangular windows high up in their blank faces, the rain sizzling off their roofs. Sheep sheltering in the lee of stone walls shook showers of drops from their fleeces like dogs. Under the flat ceiling of cloud a hundred feet overhead the Vale of Ewyas glowered moodily. But at The Vision farm, streaky fingers of weak sunshine suddenly probed through the clouds. Ruth pulled hazel nuts from the dripping hedge, and we cracked them between our teeth as the rain stopped and we walked down the glistening road into Capel-y-ffin.

FACT FILE

MAP: OS 1:50,000 Landranger Sheet 161 'Abergavenny and the Black Mountains'

TRAVEL: A465 from Abergavenny towards Hereford. Minor road at Llanvihangel Crucorney (5 miles) signed 'Llanthony'. Capel-y-ffin is 3½ miles north of Llanthony. Park by bridge.

WALK DIRECTIONS: Take side lane on right 50 yards below bridge (ref. 255314). In 200 yards go left up track to monastery (252314).

Bear left opposite Grange Farm next to monastery and climb hillside. At

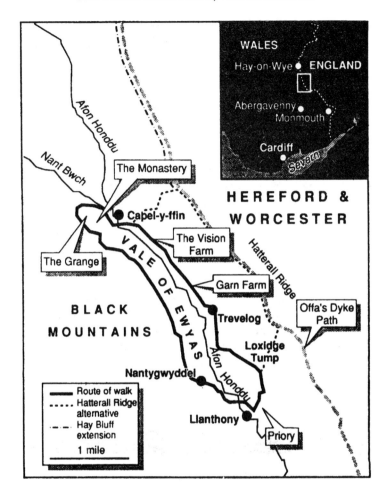

top of wood turn left on to track for 3 miles to descend to road at Nanty-gwyddel (277282). Llanthony Priory is 1 mile ahead (288278).

From Llanthony, take track behind ruins through fields to corner of wood (288286).

(a) **Hatterall Ridge route (fine weather only – avoid in mist, cloud or other bad weather conditions):** Continue steeply north up east flank of Loxidge Tump. Meet Offa's Dyke path on crest of ridge (290295) and walk north-west. Hay Bluff (244366) is 5 miles. Descend to Capel-y-ffin from ridge by steep path from 270319 to The Vision farm (265310).

(b) **Low-level hillside route:** From corner of wood, path leads along hillside, then after ¾ mile steeply down to track at Llwyn-on (279289). Continue along track to farm road just beyond Trevelog (275297), then by Garn and The Vision to Capel-y-ffin.

LENGTH OF WALK: (a) 8 miles, returning by ridge route. Allow 4 hours. Extension from 270319 to Hay Bluff and back adds 6 miles – allow extra 2–3 hours.

(b) 7 miles, returning by hillside route. Allow 3 hours.

CONDITIONS: Lanes and hill paths. Some stiff climbs and descents.

GEAR: Walking boots, waterproofs, map and compass.

REFRESHMENTS: Abbey Hotel, Llanthony

ACCOMMODATION: Abbey Hotel, Llanthony Priory (0873 890487); Court Farm, Llanthony (0873 890359); Half Moon Inn, Llanthony (0873 890611).

FURTHER READING: *Kilvert's Diary* (Penguin) – entries for 5 April, Midsummer Day and 2 September, 1870.
A Guide to Offa's Dyke Path by Christopher John Wright (Constable).

Where the Golden Eagles Dare

GLEN CLOVA AND GLEN DOLL, SCOTLAND

Pausing en route from the lushness of the Lowlands to the craggy harshness
of the Highlands south of the Grampians

For two regions with such strong individual flavours, the
Lowlands and the Highlands of Scotland share a remarkably
insubstantial border. People know which side of the line they are
on when they're *there* – but no one can draw a definitive
Lowlands/Highlands boundary across your map for you. As
good a way as any to enjoy that unmistakable shift from low to
high ground, from rolling fertility to craggy harshness of landscape, is by way of Glen Clova, a dozen miles north of Kirriemuir on the grand southerly approach to the Grampian
Mountains. At the bottom end of Glen Clova the gold and green
cornfields of Angus stretch out and away across their rich sandstone plains; but in travelling the eight miles or so to the top of
the glen you put the Lowland lushness firmly behind you and set

your face forward and up to volcanic Highland heights. As the landscape lifts, so do the spirits, in sheer elation.

My friend Dave Richardson had been up Glen Clova a couple of months before, lying on his belly in the heather of a side glen watching birds through his monoscope. Sub-arctic flora growing in crevices of the hillside had gladdened his heart, too. This sort of thing is meat and drink to Dave, an observant and informed man with whom it's always been a pleasure to walk on seashore, field or mountain. 'Might be an eagle or two around Glen Doll,' said Dave casually as we left his Edinburgh house in the morning. That remark set the day up on its hind legs.

Salmon leap along the South Esk River that wriggles through Glen Clova, and the glen itself curves like a jumping salmon up to a tail-shaped fork in the mountain buttresses at the valley's northernmost point. From the car park by the river here Glen Clova runs on northwards, while to the west Glen Doll bends off between towering rock slopes. In both glens the road sheds first tarmac, then width and smoothness, becoming the roughest of tracks heading steeply into the hills. To link the heads of the two glens over their separating saddle of trackless high ground was our aim; a really challenging task in the biting, often blinding conditions of winter in these remote passes, but a modest enough goal in the clear sunshine of late summer.

A Sunday crowd was playing family football and eating picnics in the car park, but a few hundred yards into Glen Doll all that was behind us. The track through the glen, known as Jock's Road, was for centuries a drove route, bringing the small black Highland cattle in convoys from their gathering grounds at Braemar, over the mountains and down Glen Doll to the roadside market at Callow near the foot of Glen Clova. The Jock who gave his name to this wild pathway was no drover, however; he seems to have earned a more glamorous if less respectable living as a runner or smuggler of illegally distilled whisky, carrying the mountain dew south from the stills in the Speyside glens to the thirsty folk of Kirriemuir and Dundee.

Dave and I walked fast along Jock's Road, a clinking, dusty track through the spruce and Scots pine of a Forestry Commission plantation, looking ahead over the rocket shapes of the treetops to where the Fee Burn fell whitely down the stony face of Corrie Fee. In practical terms a corrie is where the sides of a glen meet to form a steep – often a sheer – concave bowl with a rocky, clear-cut rim. In effect corries can be quite over-powering, hanging thousands of feet directly overhead with 'Thou shalt not pass' stamped implacably across them. Corrie Fee looked high enough at 2,000 feet; but what Dave told me about the plants that grow there, descendants of those that first took root in the glen shortly after the last Ice Age, softened its echoing hardness.

In this narrow side glen on his previous trip Dave had watched a golden eagle swooping down on to her nest. Today, however, the rock ledges were deserted, both around Corrie Fee and along the sides of Glen Clova. We lay beyond the trees looking through binoculars up at the scrappy twig bundle of an eagle's nest, flat on our backs on the flowery grass slopes of Glen Doll. Denied the supreme ornithological fix, we were soon nose and knee deep among the tiny plants as Dave trawled his well-barnacled botany Ph.D. memory bank for wild flower names. Grappling for nourishment in the thin soil between the fallen boulders were the miniature white stars of eyebright and the green ones of alpine lady's mantle, clumps of spicy-smelling wild thyme, pale blue harebells trembling on hair-like stalks and the flattened blue blade-shaped petals of milkwort. '*Equisetum sylvaticum*,' murmured Dave, stroking a feathery, primitive-looking green plant through his fingers, '– wood horse-tail.' The pride of the place, though, were the gentians, small and brilliantly blue against the subtle greys and greens of the glen.

Jock's Road zigzagged up the head of Glen Doll, gaining 500 feet of height in half a mile. Among the bell heather and mosses beside the path we picked wild raspberries, maybe the fruit of seeds spat out by the drovers two centuries ago – perhaps by Jock himself. At the top of the pass we paused to look back at the old road snaking down into the bottom of the glen, and the Angus hills folding and falling away to the Lowland corn plains. Up ahead, quite suddenly, the Highlands had stepped right into focus – a rocky staircase of boulders, a wilderness of barren hillsides over which a kestrel mewed and circled. We climbed laboriously up to Davy's Bourach, a dark little stone hut with a cast-iron door under a turf roof, cold and cheerless, four simple walls to shelter benighted travellers from snow and wind. Five members of the Universal Hiking Club of Glasgow had died here at New Year 1959, a memorial plaque on a rock told us. No Lowland moor could cast such a chill as this high, stark place.

Across the saddle between Glen Doll and Glen Clova, the Den of Altduthrie, we floundered among bare peat hags where red deer had wallowed and trampled the ground with their innumerable slots. Tadpoles squirmed in clotted bunches in the brown puddles of the watershed. On the rim of Glen Clova we stopped to admire the unbroken, arching sweep of the glen sides, with the peaks of Balmoral Forest rising in the distance to the shapely 3,500-foot head of Lochnagar.

We cooled our feet in the smooth, pink granite bowl of a pool, and drank Dave's thermos dry – rice tea, a faint savour of burnt toast that refreshed us for the long steep drop down the flank of Glen Clova. Through groves of twisted little birch trees we scrambled down to the track at the bottom. Back at the car park the families were still playing Dundee United versus Celtic. We left them to it, and drove slowly back down the glen into the placid, sunlit Lowlands.

FACT FILE

MAP: OS 1:50,000 Landranger Sheet 44 'Ballater and Glen Clova'

TRAVEL: From M8 Glasgow–Edinburgh motorway – Jct 1 to Forth Road Bridge; M90 to Perth; A94 to Glamis; A928 to Kirriemuir; B955 to Glen Clova, Pass Clova Hotel; car park is 4 miles further on.

WALK DIRECTIONS: From car park (284762) walk through conifer plantation into Glen Doll, following 'Jock's Road' signs. Pass Glendoll Lodge youth hostel and continue W along clear path. Fork right in 1 mile (268760), signed 'Jock's Road – Braemar 14 miles'. At end of trees go through gate (248767) and

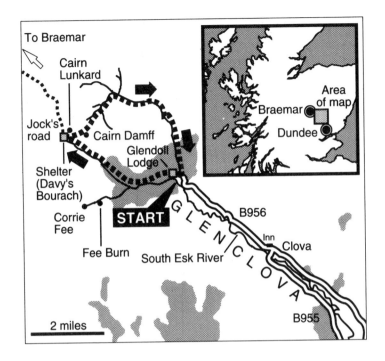

follow track up head of glen, climbing first gently and then steeply up to Davy's Bourach shelter (232778).

From shelter retrace path for 100 yards, then go left across peaty plateau of Den of Altduthrie for 1½ miles. Keep to high ground on left of western slope to pass between Cairn Lunkard (234780) and Cairn Damff (243779), aiming for slope of the latter. From Cairn Damff head N, then NE, aiming for pool on far rim of plateau.

Follow burn round to the right, NE and then ENE, to where it pours over the rim of Glen Clova (251792 approx). Go diagonally down steep glen side to join track at bottom (257794 approx); follow back to car park.

LENGTH OF WALK: 8 miles. Allow 5 hours.

CONDITIONS: Steep climb up head of Glen Doll on well-marked track. Tough going on sodden peat across plateau of Den of Altduthrie, with no clear path. Very steep, trackless descent into Glen Doll.

NB Only attempt the plateau link between the glens in clear weather. Conditions can deteriorate rapidly, even in summer, so be prepared to turn back if necessary. If caught by bad weather, shelter in Davy's Bourach. Tell someone where you are going before you set out.

GEAR: Proper hill-walking gear – hiking boots, waterproofs, extra sweater, map, compass, whistle, emergency rations.

ACCOMMODATION: Clova Hotel, Glen Clova (05755 222), also a nice stop for tea. Glendoll Lodge Youth Hostel (closes end of October) (05755 236).

Treachery, Blood and Blue Noses

THE CITY WALLS OF YORK

The great white wall of York, medieval guardian of the Minster

A cold wind was blowing a sharp hint of winter through the streets of York. Grey clouds scudded overhead, and on the upper decks of the open-topped sightseeing buses there were more blue noses than pink ones.

Striding out along the limestone parapets of York's ancient city walls, however, the whole family worked up a good warm glow under its coats and sweaters. Baby Mary in the backpack, always a sucker for anything on four legs, shouted with delight at the sight of the horse-drawn buggies and the stray dogs of York, while five-year-old Elizabeth leaped out inexhaustibly from hiding in one battlemented tower after another.

The tight circle of the medieval walls is less than three miles round, but this short stroll is weighted with history, both bloody and magnificent.

Right over the castle car park stood Clifford's Tower on its green mound, with bulging limestone walls 750 years old, built to replace a wooden keep in which 500 Jews had killed themselves back in 1190 rather than be taken and murdered by a rioting mob. It was a black note to the start of our walk, but once across the River Ouse, by way of Skeldergate Bridge, we were up and away along the walls.

No half-crumbled snippets of masonry, these city walls of York, but an almost complete circle of hard magnesian limestone, a creamy-white ribbon of battlemented stone drawn close around York's red brick houses, half-timbered shops and church towers and spires crammed shoulder to shoulder along narrow roadways.

Below us the pavements were packed with tourists and early Christmas shoppers, even at this tail-end of autumn; but filtered through a lattice of gold and green horse-chestnut leaves the city lay low and quiet, less substantial than the 700-year-old stone footway beneath our shoes. The pinnacles and great square towers of York Minster added to this dreamy feeling.

The walls are pierced by four great stone gateways or bars, whose frowning solidity is best appreciated from down at road level, reached by narrow, dark and steep stairways. We came first to Micklegate Bar, facing south-west down the London road; fourteenth-century towers on Norman bases through whose archways the traffic grinds slowly.

There were cheery notices outside exhorting us not to pass by without entering the tiny stone rooms of the Bar. Wooden ladders led precariously up to a top-floor exhibition of enthusiastically executed paintings. Another cheery notice explained the lack of anything more historical up here; it wouldn't be fair on those who couldn't manage the stairs.

Throughout the Middle Ages traitors' heads were spiked and displayed on the top of Micklegate Bar, the last two (those of a couple of Bonnie Prince Charlie's supporters) as recently as 1754. All but one of the outward-thrusting barbicans or defensive courtyards of York's gateways were pulled down in the 1820s and 30s. Sir Walter Scott offered to walk from Edinburgh to York if the city corporation would agree to spare Micklegate's barbican, but in vain; Progress and the Free Flow of Traffic were not to be thwarted.

From Micklegate Bar the curling ribbon of the wall led north, dipping down in successive snake bends towards the River Ouse and Lendal Bridge.

Suddenly, York Minster stood squarely ahead in all its glory, anchored to earth beyond the river.

Across the river at Lendal Tower (once the pumping station which squeezed Ouse water through oaken pipes to the households of York) the wall vanished, leaving us to detour through the Museum Gardens and by the soaring arches of St Mary's Abbey ruins. We passed the lumpy blocks of the Multangular Tower, its Roman masonry and tilework intact up to twenty feet above the ground, to emerge from the Gardens opposite Bootham Bar, the second of York's great gateways.

The Bar straddles the road that brought Roman soldiers into their fortress of Eboracum. These days the view from ground level is of the squat old gateway guarding red brick walls and slate roofs in a jumble of geometry, the towers of the Minster sailing calmly behind and over all.

Beyond Bootham Bar the Minster grows in height and bulk as it stands sideways-on to the footway along the walls, soaring superbly above the tranquil green gardens of the Deanery. A fine crop of cabbages was growing in the Dean's walled garden, sheltered from the increasing bite of the wind that was now sweeping through the parapets. A blue nose appeared in the backpack; another peeped out in ambush round the next corner. Time for the rest of the expedition to peel off in search of teacakes, hot chocolate and shops full of Christmas presents.

Stepping out briskly on my own, I clattered down and up the steep stairways of the tall Monk Bar, on whose top stood carved figures threatening to throw the stones they clutched down on to the heads of attackers below. Outside the wall beyond the Bar huddled the domed brick roof of York's old Ice House, built here in about 1800 to hold layers of ice packed in straw. Collected and stored each winter, the ice would stay frozen until dug out for refrigeration duty the following summer.

Now the walk's surroundings began to take on a less ancient look as the wall ran down to disappear on the corner of a busy road junction. The route continued along Foss Islands Road – 'the least inviting stretch of the circuit' apologized my guide booklet – but I rather enjoyed this short stretch between factories and the duck-haunted, willow-fringed, dark ditch of the River Foss.

Here William the Conqueror had had the river dammed to make a lake known as the King's Pool; hence the gap in the wall at this point. At the turn of the road stood the stumpy little Red Tower, brick-built as a lookout post in 1490. Beyond it the wall reappeared to curve round to Walmgate Bar.

The barbican here has survived eight centuries of assault by attackers and developers. Sticking out into the roadway in front of the gate, it masks the full height of the Bar itself, and robs it of that air of blank-faced grimness worn by York's other great gateways.

At the tall tower of Fishergate Postern a few hundred yards further on, I climbed down from the wall for the last time and walked round the curve of York Castle's Georgian wall. Elegant enough in itself, it concealed until the last moment the far more dramatic walls of Clifford's Tower above the car park. A suitably grand and historic end to the walk – though still in prospect was a sticky reunion embrace from a now warm and chocolate-coated Mary.

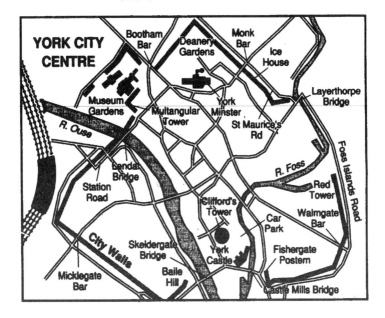

MAP: OS 1:50,000 Landranger Sheet 105 'York'

Large-scale town map is more use: available from the Tourist Information Office at De Grey Rooms, Exhibition Square (0904 621756) and York Station (0904 643700).

Excellent booklet with detailed information and historical notes in *Walking the Walls*, also from Tourist Information Offices.

TRAVEL: By road from south, A1 and A64; from north, A1 and A59. Car park at York Castle.

By rail to York Station.

WALK DIRECTIONS: From Castle car park (605514) walk past Clifford's Tower and over Skeldergate Bridge (603513) to join the wall circuit at Baile Hill. No direction-finding problems from here on – just follow the footway.

From Lendal Bridge (600520) walk up Museum Street, turning left in 100 yards into Museum Gardens. Follow path to Multangular Tower; bear right out of Gardens to Bootham Bar (602523). Continue circuit to Monk Bar, and on to the next gap in wall where St Maurice's Road meets Layerthorpe Bridge (608521) – busy blind corner, so take care emerging from gateway.

Cross bridge and continue down Foss Islands Road to pick up wall again at Red Tower (610518). Continue to Walmgate Bar and Fishergate Postern (607513). Keep ahead here over Castle Mills Bridge to skirt York Castle and return to car park.

LENGTH OF WALK: 2½ miles – can be done in less than an hour, but allow at least two to appreciate it.

CONDITIONS: Some steep, narrow flights of steps to street level; some steps in footway itself; many unguarded drops of up to 20 feet. These make the walk unsuitable for unruly small children and for disabled or infirm people.

GEAR: Ordinary outdoor clothes and footwear, but wrap up warmly.

REFRESHMENTS: Many excellent pubs and cafés in York.

ACCOMMODATION: Many hotels in and out of York. The whole family was very comfortable and felt welcome at Knavesmire Manor, 302 Tadcaster Road, York YO2 2HE (0904 702941).

FURTHER READING: *Illustrated Portrait of York* by Ronald Willis (Robert Hale)

Breezy Bredon

BREDON HILL, WORCESTERSHIRE

The summit of Bredon Hill, the Hereford & Worcester
landmark made famous by the poet Housman

'Now, then – who's coming for a walk up Bredon Hill?' That
was the penalty clause at the end of the Christmas lunches
of my Gloucestershire childhood. Bow-legged with brandy butter and crystallized fruits, there was only one acceptable remedy
– over the border into Worcestershire, and straight up Bredon.

Eyes would unglaze, spinning heads clear and tight
stomachs relax as the forced march went forward, until what
had been a painful effort at the bottom of Bredon became more
of a scamper the higher we climbed. Anyone and everyone
turned out – baby sisters, friends of parents, friends of friends.
Even Uncle Arthur, dapper and gentle (but with a taste for
sandwiching half an inch of mustard into his beef that made my
eyes water just to see), would stump on his eighty-year-old legs
up the lower reaches.

Bredon Hill rises to nine hundred feet, a long dome crowned with trees and striped with hedges and stone walls, swelling from the flat vale of the River Avon. The hill serves as a visual anchor for this whole border region of Gloucestershire and Worcestershire. Everyone for miles around knows Bredon, having its familiar green bulk as a reference point in their everyday geography. And climbing the hill you can orientate yourself in sixty or seventy miles of country spread out with its rivers, roads, towns and hill ranges like a gigantic relief map at your feet – a eupeptic panorama to settle the hash of any rebellious Christmas pudding.

Little villages of golden stone, thatch and black-and-white timbering lie in a snug ring around the skirts of Bredon Hill; Elmley Castle, Ashton-under-Hill, Overbury, Kemerton, Bredon's Norton. There are ways up on to the hill from each of these – overgrown sheep tracks, old cart roads, bridleways, neatly waymarked footpaths. One day this winter we set out to hurdle Bredon from the west and end up on the east side of the hill at Ashton; not to work down a Christmas lunch, but to work up a decent appetite.

We climbed the steep road through the little hamlet of Westmancote, between Kemerton and Bredon's Norton, on a breezy morning of quick weather changes between the gloomiest black clouds and the most brilliant sunshine. When the sun came through to strike the stony track above the hamlet, it brought out the buttery yellow of Bredon's oolitic limestone in all its beauty. Deeply scored by water channels that soon turn into miniature torrents after heavy rainfall, the wide old cart track went gently uphill between hedges dotted with blood-red rosehips and draped with lacy mats of old-man's-beard. Riders came skittering down the hill, their mounts digging in hooves and sending up showers of yellow, crumbly stone.

The quarries that once scarred the flanks of Bredon are silent nowadays. One or two of the biggest are still not really safe to explore, but up here beside the bridleway the old delvings have greened over into hummocky slopes, their little hillocks and dells making ideal hide-and-seek places for energetic toddlers. The pair on Bredon with us today rolled and tumbled their appetites into life, while their seniors sat and gazed out west and south over the great flat plain where the Rivers Avon and Severn snaked past church spires and under the faintly roaring M5 motorway; out past the indigo-shadowed dinosaur spine of the Malvern Hills ten miles away, and over another thirty or forty miles to distant pale blue lumps across the Welsh border – the Black Mountains and Brecon Beacons.

Sheep were feeding on the stubble and root vegetable leaves, and the youngest member of our party got down on her hands and knees with every intention of doing the same. What with sheep, horses and the pheasants that kok-kokked echoingly inside walled plantations by the path, there was enough zoological zest to entice the toddlers a little further up Bredon.

There's a growing sense of something stupendous in the way of views somewhere not far ahead, as the bridleway climbs towards a line of gnarled old oaks. Then suddenly it's there, bang on the edge of a steep drop with scores of miles in prospect between the bare branches, sweeping north towards the Midlands and away west past the sprawl of Worcester (the cathedral standing out, tiny but clear) to the hard volcanic peaks of the Clee Hills nearly forty miles off.

Breathtaking as it is at this elevation, the real glory of the Bredon view is only to be tasted by those who trek on and up through the old oaks and beeches to the pre-Roman settlement of Bredon Camp at the summit of the hill. Here by the folly tower, at over nine hundred feet, you stare all round the completed circle – Brecons and Black Mountains in the south-west, Malverns and Clees out west; Midland plains and low, rolling ridges far to the north; nearer at hand the noble Cotswold uplands and outliers swooping up and away above Cheltenham in the south and east. From horizon to horizon there can't be much less than a hundred miles on view here. So dizzying is the sense of height and distance that it's almost with relief that one turns along the camp ramparts to find the Cotswolds close in front, the villages at their feet looking near enough to reach down and touch.

Tiring of the bridleway's mud and ruts, I navigated the whole party into trouble along what turned out to be the longest of short cuts. Lalu Farm is a lonely place at the crest of Bredon where house and barn form a right angle of solid stonework that defies wind and weather from the shelter of a belt of immense beech trees. Here the farmer put us right; then I put us wrong again. Stick to that bridleway, is my advice with hindsight. However, there was one personal treat which the right path would have missed out – a view down the broad grass track that leads off the hill to Overbury. This was the return route of the family's Christmas afternoon walks on Bredon, usually trodden on weary feet, with chilled hands deep in pockets and eyes fixed forward on a huge, smoky-red sun sinking inch by inch down through the interlacing twigs of the bare beech trees.

A bit of common sense (from someone else) put us on the bridleway again, skimming the edge of Bredon's north-eastern slope and dropping down over deeply trenched ridge-and-furrow ground, remnant of medieval strip-farming by the peasants of Ashton-under-Hill. There are heavily laden orchards above the half-timbered old houses of Ashton, a part-Norman church well worth exploring, and an excellent pub, The Star. A car, prudently parked here before the start of the walk, stood ready to take us all back to Westmancote. But first, while the two ten-leagues-under toddlers snored in their backpacks in mild sunshine, there was time for a lunch in the pub's garden of which Uncle Arthur would have thoroughly approved – plenty of beef, and plenty of mustard.

FACT FILE

MAP: OS 1:50,000 Landranger Sheet 150 'Worcester and The Malverns'

TRAVEL: M5 to Jct 9; A438 for 2 miles to Aston Cross; left on B4079 towards Bredon; in 3 miles, right on minor road to Westmancote. Continue over crossroads; park at top of road.

WALK DIRECTIONS: Walk on up road, which becomes wide track. At fork (946384) bear left and keep to bridleway up hill. At top of rise in 1½ miles

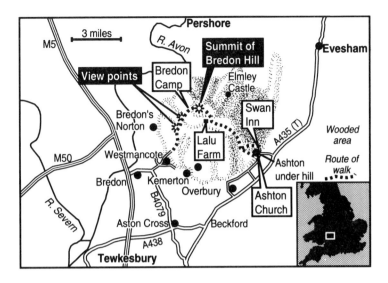

(948397) turn right and continue for 1 mile to tower and Bredon Camp at summit of hill (957401). Carry on along bridleway for 1 mile to top corner of wood (967403); turn right here and keep to edge of wood for 1 mile until bridleway leaves wood (977395) and begins to lose height. In 1¼ miles bridleway joins another at footpath fingerpost (986384). Either bear left and snake downhill to north end of Ashton-under-Hill, or go through gate by fingerpost and continue down hollow in hillside and over waymarked stiles to reach church (997377), hidden by knoll until last moment.

NB: There are many paths up Bredon Hill from points all round the base, and excellent round walks of any length can easily be worked out from the map.

LENGTH OF WALK: 5 miles – allow 3 hours for uphill walking and stops to enjoy the views.

CONDITIONS: Uphill section is not demanding, but bridleway can be muddy after rain. Suitable for all the family, but take backpack for under-4s.

GEAR: Strong boots for the muddy sections; windproof clothing for the heights, especially at the summit. Encouraging snacks and drinks for young children are recommended!

23

REFRESHMENTS: The Star Inn, Ashton-under-Hill – a few yards north of church.

ACCOMMODATION: Beckford Inn, Beckford, Nr Evesham, Worcs. (0386 881254)

FURTHER READING: *The Distant Scene, The Secrets Of Bredon Hill* and other books by Fred Archer, local writer of Ashton-under-Hill – available at Post Office, Ashton.

Brensham Village by John Moore (Collins, 1946) – set in Bredon

'Summertime on Bredon' by A. E. Housman (Poem xxi, *A Shropshire Lad*)

Lonely Old Port in a Storm

ORFORD, SUFFOLK

The River Ore runs inside a shingle spit, which stretches six miles south-west from Orford, cutting it off from the sea

Driving towards Orford across the heath, I could tell it was going to be a cold and windy walk. Out over the North Sea snow clouds were hanging in smoky folds above a lemon-yellow strip of sky, and the conifers on the heath were thrashing their tops together. A good strong gale with sleet and snow showers, driving abnormally high tides before it, was due to hit the Suffolk coast some time that morning, and judging by the agitated trees and the scudding grey sky its vanguard had already arrived. The twin towers of Orford's castle and church stood high over the little red-roofed village at the end of the road against a background of purple clouds, lit brilliantly by a last gleam of sunshine defying the enveloping storm.

Down on Orford Quay there was a complete absence of activity. A solitary elderly man in tall boots and a blue sailor's cap stood watching the swollen waters of the River Ore lapping his front doorstep. 'It do this four or five times a year,' he ruminated, dabbing his boot-tip in the flood. 'The river come up and visit us. Soon go, though.'

No one else was about, on the quay or in the wide single street of the village that runs down to the river. Orford in winter is a quiet place, isolated at the end of its long road from Wood-bridge on the tip of the lonely peninsula between the River Ore and the Butley River. In medieval times it was a thriving and bustling coastal port, trading in wool, thronged with ships, sailors and merchants. But the East Coast tides played their familiar trick on Orford, building up a bank of shingle that extended southward year by year, blocking off the sea approaches and choking the harbour with silt. 'Orford was once a good town, but is decayed,' noted Daniel Defoe in 1722. 'The sea daily throws up more land to it, and falls off itself from it, as if it was resolved to disown the place, and that it should be a sea port no longer.'

Nowadays the shingle spit stretches six miles south-west from the village, the River Ore curving inside its long barrier. Only the great castle keep, the size and beauty of the church and the touches of Dutch influence in the curly gables of houses in Orford bear witness to the prosperous centuries of trading up and down the coast and across the North Sea.

On the far side of the river a red-and-white-striped light-house stands on Orford Ness, the bulging elbow where the spit bends south and west. 'Can't get over there now,' said the old man on the quay. 'There used to be a ferry, but that's all MoD these days.' He pulled up his collar against a stinging burst of sleet slanting in from the sea, and watched me squelching off along the muddy path on top of the river's flood wall. At a bend in the wall I looked back to see him still moodily kicking the tideline like an Orford Canute, the only occupant of the deserted quay.

Through binoculars I made out a scattering of military excrescences on the shingle bar across the Ore – stark huts, mounds, posts draped with wire. The spit is all but inaccessible from Orford, barred to the public by water and wire. Among the MoD buildings were ornithologists' netted bird traps. Orford Ness is a major landfall for birds on migration from across the North Sea. Many of them find safe haven on the RSPB refuge of Havergate Island, a slab of mud and marsh that fills a wide lagoon in the river here.

The broad surface of the Ore was roughened like fish skin by the wind, with a dull, greasy gleam where the sun shone weakly behind the snow clouds. I found a seat just above the tideline, with the flood wall as a windbreak behind my head, and scanned the flat snout of Havergate Island through the glasses. Turnstones were picking over the bladderwrack dumped by the morning's high tide; oyster-catchers piped out of long scarlet bills; a flight of small waders – knot? dunlin? I wasn't sharp enough to tell – carved a flight path low across the Ore with white-streaked scimitar wings, swerving all together at the same split second.

No avocets, though. They must have been off on their West Country winter break on the Tamar estuary. The RSPB logo is an avocet, and no wonder. Plumage-seekers and egg-collectors had wiped out avocets as a breeding species in this country by 1825. The reappearance and subsequent breeding of the blue-legged, black-and-white wading bird with the upturned bill is one of the RSPB's biggest success stories. The avocets chose Havergate Island just after the war, the RSPB bought it, and the birds have bred here on and off ever since.

The gale was working itself up into a worsening mood. As I came up from the shelter of the flood wall the wind ploughed the river into long white furrows, and put a cold hand in my back to shove me along the path. The RSPB wardens' boat swayed at its moorings off Havergate Island. I hunched my shoulders and scurried along round Chantry Point, up to where a footpath left the river to cross the fields to the Orford road.

The view ahead changed from the flatness of water, salting and shingle to the flatness of arable land reclaimed from the sea by the Austin Friars of medieval Orford. The drainage ditches were lined with swans in hiding from the coming storm, heads under wings. The fresh salt and mud smell of the tidal river gave way to fruity wafts of silage from Richmond Farm, lying low in a huddle of red brick and tile. The wind roared in the bare branches of the trees round the farm. Looking back beyond the marsh fields I had a glimpse of the open sea, a thin silver bar laid along the top of the dull brown strip of the shingle spit.

Orford Castle stood on the edge of the village, the very image of how a castle keep ought to look with corner towers, little arched windows and soaring walls on a great ridged mound. A flag streamed bravely over the battlements. Orford Castle was built from 1165 to 1171 for King Henry II, with an eighteen-sided central keep which was a revolutionary design in its day. The strangest inmate in the castle's long history was a 'guest' there just after it was built – a naked merman, wild and hairy, who had been netted by the Orford fishermen. He was hung upside down and tortured in the castle in a vain attempt to get him to talk. But the silent merman slipped through his captors' hands and back into the sea again. That's the story, anyway.

Spiral stairs inside the keep led me up past cylindrical rooms hung with maps of Orford in times past, and out on to the roof. There was a superb view over the village and back along the river, marshes, island and shingle spit. But up here, ninety feet above the ground, the wind was a battering ram that bundled me back into the tower and down the stairs, throwing a spray of snow after me for good measure.

Over the road, the wide interior of St Bartholomew's Church rattled and sighed in the gale. Here in 1958 Benjamin Britten's *Noye's Fludde* had its first performance, followed in 1964 by his *Curlew River*. Orford lies just to the south of what the local tourist board has not yet got round to calling 'Britten Country'. Snape Maltings are five miles north of Orford, Aldeburgh the other side of the river where the shingle spit starts. Britten conjured some of his best music from these windy marshlands.

Back at the quay the tide was still rising. The landlord of the Jolly Sailor looked worried and talked of coastguard warnings and sandbags. Snowflakes hurtled past the windows of the pub, but I was on the right side of the glass. The stove threw out heat. A trio of old ladies at lunch gave each other the local news at top volume in extra strong Suffolk accents. A pint of equally power-ful, locally brewed Adnams bitter stood within reach. I looked at the map. Another few miles, along the river and into 'Britten Country'? To hell with that!

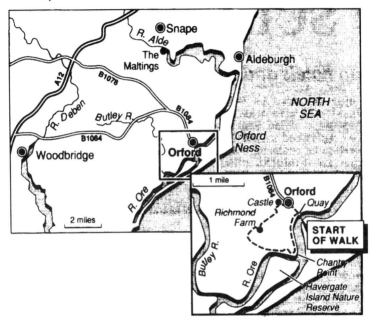

FACT FILE

MAP: OS 1:50,000 Landranger Sheets 169 'Ipswich and the Naze' and 156 'Saxmundham and Aldeburgh'

TRAVEL: From south – A12 to Woodbridge, then A1152 and B1084. From north – A12 to Wickham Market, then B1078 and B1084. Car park at Orford Quay.

WALK DIRECTIONS: From Orford Quay (425495), bear right and follow flood wall of River Ore for 1½ miles around Chantry Point and inland to public footpath sign 'Richmond and Orford' (415485), Green track leads to road (409490); turn right for 1 mile to reach Orford Castle (419499).

LENGTH OF WALK: 3 miles – allow 2 hours for bird watching and castle climbing.

CONDITIONS: Path can be muddy, but otherwise an easy, level stroll.

GEAR: Boots; plenty of warm clothes on this exposed coast; binoculars; bird book.

REFRESHMENTS AND ACCOMMODATION: The Jolly Sailor, Orford Quay (0394 450243)

FURTHER READING: *Orford, Suffolk* – booklet by Jean and Stuart Bacon, available from castle kiosk

LISTENING: *Noye's Fludde, Curlew River* or *Peter Grimes*, all by Benjamin Britten

Bright Lights, Gothic Gloom

BANKSIDE, LONDON

The murky Thames heaves beneath Blackfriars railway bridge,
with the dome of St Paul's rising beyond

The Thames hadn't changed much in twenty years – the water itself, I mean. Sluggishly heaving beneath the crimson bows of Blackfriars Bridge, it looked just as murkily mysterious as ever. My mind's eye still scattered its muddy bed with iron-bound chests of plundered jewels and the corpses of one-eyed Lascar seamen, symbols of the dreadful fascination laid on the river by Sherlock Holmes and Bill Sikes. For me – and for many another non-Londoner, I suspect – the Thames still flows through a sinister fantasy of opium dens, gas-lit alleys and muffled splashes under trap doors.

Victorian atmosphere had clung thickly to the Thames when I last walked its waterfront in the early 1970s, from Tower Bridge to Limehouse. In Wapping High Street the faintest of spicy smells – cinnamon, ginger, cloves – still wafted from the crumbling warehouses, and slimy steps led down between great gloomy walls to where the tide swirled round rotting wooden jetties. But something had happened to the Thames since then; a change of face glimpsed from time to time on occasional London visits, but never properly taken in till now. Where were the tottering, grimy warehouses, the rows of broken windows, the shabby acres? I gazed from Blackfriars Bridge at the new shapes planted on the river bank – buildings like window blinds on end, like 1920s racing cars, like moored liners. No nourishment here for Dickensian nightmares.

Steps led down from the southern end of the bridge to a path raised high along the river wall. I turned east and headed past the Founders Arms into a bitter wind. How snug the drinkers looked on the warm side of the windows. Down on the tideline black-headed gulls were scavenging the leavings of the city. Against the grey mud and green pebbles the gulls looked trim and, considering the toxicity of their feeding ground, remarkably healthy in their winter plumage, the chocolate head colour of summer faded to a tiny smudge of black behind the eye, red legs stalking and red beaks stabbing in the soft foreshore. They hopped nonchalantly over the old landing stairs and cobbled hards exposed by the falling tide.

Two cormorants stood motionless on the poles of an ancient landing stage a few yards out in the water. A train of three rusty old barges went chopping by in mid-river. On the north bank, above the green and gold polaroid windows of the new office blocks, St Paul's dome stood out proudly. This was more like it.

The redundant Bankside Power Station scowled over the riverside path, cold and lightless, tiny vertical strips of window seaming its great dull face. The wind trembled the old flagpole on the roof. An enormous square chimney tapered towards the clouds. In the shadow of the giant brick walls two lovers were generating their own power on a bench. Their activity against the phallic upthrust of the chimney would have made a superb photograph, but I didn't have the heart to frame them.

Beyond the power station stood a little fragment of old London, a tall Queen Anne house on a scrap of cobbled street not yet buried under concrete. In the house's name, Cardinal's Wharf, is caught a whole slice of history. Here was the wharf where Catherine of Aragon, only sixteen years old but already a widow, landed in 1502. Her dead fourteen-year-old husband, Prince Arthur, had been heir to the English throne, and soon she was to be married off to his handsome, athletic younger brother, Prince Henry. History certainly had some nasty shocks in store for poor Catherine, as her dashing prince bloated, coarsened, turned into Henry VIII and divorced her.

The plaque on the house wall says that Catherine took shelter here after landing, probably in the inn called the Cardinal's Hatte that stood on the site then. The plaque also claims, rather more dubiously, that Sir Christopher Wren stayed here while rebuilding St Paul's. If so, he had a marvellous view of each stage of his achievement across the river. The needle's-eye passageway of Cardinal's Cap Alley runs down the side of Cardinal's Wharf, and from its depths I looked out to see the cathedral dome framed in the dark chink of the alley's entrance.

At one time in its chequered history the Cardinal's Hatte was a well-known brothel, one of a whole string along this southern stretch of the Thames. Many a young blade's night on the town would end with a transpontine visit to the Bankside stews. And among the bawdy houses stood the round wooden theatres of Tudor times – the Swan, the Rose, the Hope and William Shakespeare's own Globe. Beyond Cardinal's Wharf I skirted a hole in the face of Bankside, where a reconstruction of the Globe is under way – a bold project.

I turned off down Bear Gardens Lane between high black warehouse walls where weeds sprouted from drainpipes and roof ledges. Here both the fine and the foul folk of Tudor and Stuart London came to watch mastiffs, bulls and bears tearing and tossing each other. There's quieter entertainment in the Bear Gardens today at the Shakespeare Globe Museum, where a mighty stuffed bear stands guard over an exhibition showing how both Globe and Rose theatres were recently unearthed. In Park Street below Bear Gardens Lane I begged a quick glance behind the security fencing at the original site of the Globe, a wasteland of weed-grown foundations and scummy pools opposite the gleaming new *Financial Times* building.

The east wind off the river nipped harder at my nose as I

came level with the Anchor Inn in the shadow of the railway bridge over to Cannon Street. City workers were opening the doors into the glow and cheery roar of the bars, peeling off their overcoats with an 'aaah' of warmth. Get thee behind me for the moment, Young's and Courage's. I rubbed my blue fingers to get the blood moving and went on under the bridge into Clink Street, a perfect scene from my private Thames-side fantasy. All the terror and mystery of Shadwell and Wapping, Bermondsey and Rotherhithe, coalesced along this narrow roadway snaking between stark bastions of warehouse walls, their windows barred, their gantries, chains and pulleys creaking as they swung in the wind overhead: daylight shut out, passers-by shut in.

But Gothic gloom was quickly dispelled down in the bowels of the Clink. A strange effect, considering the grim history of this ancient prison which held debtors, whores, thieves, murderers, martyrs and madmen from Norman until Georgian times. A dingy doorway led into the old gaol, nowadays housing an exhibition of the Clink story. The owner was getting the place ready for a party, but he let me wander round among the torture tools, the gibbets and manacles. The party was to be held in the 'explicit' room – 'only one in the world, mate,' said the owner with pride – hung with prints of fat ladies in mob caps being spanked and gentlemen caught doing up their breeches. I hope it was a good thrash.

All this land south of the Thames belonged to the medieval Bishops of Winchester, Clink prison included. A few yards further along Clink Street I looked up to see the large and beautiful rose window of the bishops' Winchester Palace, delicate stone tracery that has looked down on six hundred years of Bankside life, rich and rowdy. At the end of Clink Street in the little inlet of St Mary Overy's Dock lay the old black topsail schooner *Kathleen & May*, and beyond her loomed the dark, flint-studded flanks of Southwark Cathedral.

Notwithstanding all the changes that modern office development has brought to Bankside, the cathedral still dominates its own small area, with a feeling of space and stillness both inside and out. In spite of constant rebuilding over its 900-year history, it looks wonderfully complete and all of a piece. Behind the altar is the retro-choir, a cool stone forest of slender pillars and overarching branches of fan vaulting. You can pick your own favourite monument from a whole treasury; mine are a balding and dreamy-looking Shakespeare with old Bankside in relief behind him, and the memorial to Joyce Austin in the north transept that features two painted haymakers with pitchfork and rake, disconsolately sobbing under broad-brimmed straw hats.

Out under the steely grey sky again, I heeded (like Mole in 'Dulce Domum') the irresistible summons of the Anchor's warmth and light. But before turning my back to the wind I climbed up on to London Bridge for a last look east along the river, past Tower Bridge and down to where the bright tinted glass of the new age mirrored the last sombre monoliths of the Thames of Dickens and Doyle.

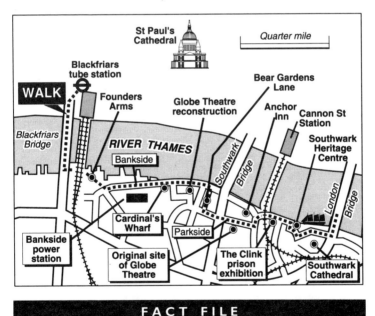

FACT FILE

MAP: Best map, and full information, in booklet *The Story of Bankside*, from Southwark Heritage Visitor Centre (*see below*)
London A–Z pages 61a, 61b

TRAVEL: Blackfriars tube (District and Circle lines)

WALK DIRECTIONS: Cross Blackfriars Bridge, turn left, keep going!

LENGTH OF WALK: I mile approx – allow 2 hours for exhibitions and exploring.

REFRESHMENTS: Founders Arms and Anchor Inn, Bankside; Chapter House Restaurant in Southwark Cathedral (closed weekends) for good, cheap food.

EXHIBITIONS: Shakespeare Globe Museum, Bear Gardens Lane (Mon–Sat 10–5, Sun 2–5); Clink Exhibition (7 days a week); *Kathleen & May* schooner, St Mary Overy's Dock (Mon–Fri).

FURTHER INFORMATION: Southwark Heritage Visitor Centre, St Mary Overy's Dock, Cathedral Street, SE1 (071 407 5911).

Snow-White and the
Severn Wharves

LITTLETON-ON-SEVERN, AVON

The broad Severn estuary widens towards the spidery cradle
of the Severn Bridge

It was a satisfying noise; *c-r-r-ack!* The milky skin of ice over
the tractor rut split across into a web of fine lines, splintered
into glassy shards and caved in under my boot. I hadn't heard
that tearing little explosion for three mild winters in a row, and
now it brought a flood of childhood memories – breaking into
one frozen ditch after another for the sheer pleasure of shat-
tering virgin ice. I crunched ten yards of ice, grinning like a fool,
before sliding on out of the gateway and into the frosty silence of
the fields.

Between Welsh hills and flat English meadows the River
Severn breaks free from its miles of tortuous winding and surges
beneath the Severn Bridge to meet the wide, muddy waters of

the Bristol Channel. The English bank hereabouts, just upriver of the bridge, is undramatic countryside of tree-topped knolls rising gently from barely rolling fields. Its landmarks stand up emphatically by contrast – a red-roofed barn, an oak in the hedgerow, the swoop and curve of the great bridge on the southern skyline.

Setting off from Littleton-on-Severn among its deep-ditched lanes, I had found myself hemmed in by snow-powdered hedges and fields from which a white sky had drained every drop of colour and perspective. But up here on the ridge above the village the view broadened as a pale disc of sun swam behind the clouds, bringing some depth and tone to the scene.

A shaft of sunlight slipped through to spotlight a red tractor on the opposite slope half a mile away, where two tiny figures, black against the snow, bent and straightened over some frozen-fingered task. Beyond them, hidden by the angle of the hill but powerfully sensed, lay the mighty curve of the River Severn, broadening out in its final few landbound miles. I looked back to see the spidery cradle of the Severn Bridge, its distant foot planted on the Welsh shore whose snowy hills ran parallel with the river, the weak sunlight brushing them with a rosy glow.

Hands clenched deep in anorak pockets and neck well hunched into scarf, I trudged through fluffy snow, aiming for the red roof of St Arilda's Church perched on a knoll ahead. In the whitened fields there was never a hint of the footpath shown on the map, but the beeline took me over thorn hedges and through a cider apple orchard whose owner, pruning knife in numb fingers and breath steaming like a kettle, called hello from the top of her ladder.

The path crossed in front of a farmhouse, past old washing steps in the stream bank, to meet a road. St Arilda's beckoned from its little tump, but when I climbed up the sagging stone steps I found the porch screen padlocked. Screams of children playing in the schoolyard below cut the air with that characteristic hard ring of frosty weather. I took a sight on the distant gleam of the Severn and plodded off down the slushy lane from Cowhill that dog-legs towards the river bank.

Old orchards are a feature of this Severn Valley landscape, and in one of them I found strange fruit under the trees – trumpet-shaped skeletons woven of withies or willow twigs, six feet long and stacked into tall towers. They looked like the framework of half-finished carnival dragons. 'Putchers,' said the farmer's wife at the orchard gate, popping out of her house to see what I might be up to. 'Salmon traps. He's the only one around here making them these days. Goes down to the Somerset Levels for his withies. It has to be withy, otherwise they fall to pieces when they're lifted out of the water. They'll be in the river come Easter.'

Across the lane in a boggy dell grew a little plantation of withies, whippy twigs sprouting like whiskers from the tops of stumpy pollarded willows a couple of feet tall. Each twig was streaked with gold by the wintry sun, but there was no warmth in those pale rays. I left a trail of mashed ice fragments behind me in the ruts, stamping my way in childish glee past the farms and down the lane between frost-rimed hedges. A snipe jinked up and away from a patch of sodden ground as yet unfrozen. Under the snow the fields rippled with the corrugations of medieval ridge-and-furrow farming.

Ahead the long line of the flood wall blocked off what lay beyond, a gigantic view all the more exciting for the suddenness of its unrolling. As soon as I topped the grassy wall the broad Severn burst out and away to north and south, two miles wide, an eddying highway of sweeping, tide-tugged water racing down to the sea, all sinewy strength and purposeful movement. Mud banks were rolling clear of the falling tide, each one packed with feeding birds – Canada geese, cormorants, oyster-catchers, a flock of two or three hundred wigeon that got up with a tremendous clatter the moment my head came above the flood wall.

Mysterious frameworks of poles stood out into the tide, some marking the place where those putchers would be stationed for the spring run of salmon, others of unguessable significance. Frozen rings of salt encrusted the little mud bays at the marshy edge of the river. Suddenly the world had widened into a heady mix of salty smells, water movement and bird clamour. It was as if I had been walking in suspense, waiting for just this magical moment.

Two miles downriver the Severn Bridge crawled with slow-moving, soundless traffic, its English end bedded into the top of a dusky red sandstone cliff. The thread-like bow of the bridge had drawn my gaze throughout the walk; but here on the tideline among the ducks and wading birds, the prints of fox and rabbit in the snow-filled marsh gullies, it seemed only one element in a scene both frozen and full of life.

In the White Hart at Littleton-on-Severn I thawed out over beef pie and a pint of Smiles's Bristol-brewed ale. Ancient settles, dark old wood panelling and staircase, mullioned windows, stone-flagged floors, a blazing fire – the White Hart was just what the doctor ordered to bring back blood to the system and a contented glaze to the eye. Where the children's room is fitted out with as much easy thoughtfulness as the bars, you can be sure the pub's a gem.

In the bar I asked about the signpost I'd seen, labelled 'Whale Wharf'. The landlord handed over a much-thumbed version of the tale. Back in 1895 a whale had beached below Littleton, 'sixty eaight feet long' according to the diary kept by Hector Knapp, a local fisherman who had been to see the beast. 'The Whal bid thear a fortnight. Thear supposed to be forty thousen pepeal to se it from all parts of the cuntry.'

The little group of Littletonians round the bar watched the inquisitive stranger reading with quiet amusement.

'We still call it Whale Warf,' someone said when I'd finished. 'That's the most exciting thing that's ever happened down here, you know.'

FACT FILE

MAP: OS 1:50,000 Landranger Sheet 172 'Bristol and Bath'

TRAVEL: From south and north, M5 to Jct 16; from east and west, M4 to Jct 20, M5 to Jct 16. A38 north from Jct 16 for 4 miles to Alveston: B4461 west for

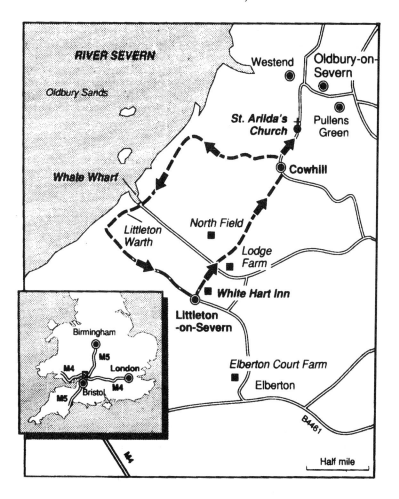

3 miles to Elberton; minor road on right to Littleton-on-Severn (1½ miles). Park car at White Hart.

WALK DIRECTIONS: Turn right from White Hart (596900) and walk north up lane to triangular green (597903). On far side, footpath fingerpost points beside 'Hollyhocks' (long white house) over stile and through tiny orchard. Aim half-right and over gate for corner of wood on skyline (602905). From here make for red roof of St Arilda's Church on knoll ahead (609919). On far side of big field, path goes through gate into orchard, and bears right between farmhouse and stream to gate into lane (606914).

Keep ahead to reach St Arilda's; bear left at No Through Road sign down lane (606915) for 1 mile to reach River Severn (594918). Turn left and follow flood wall for 1 mile, past industrial buildings at Whale Wharf (589910) and on to gate on your left (583907) leading to foot of lane (585905), which runs back in 1 mile to Littleton.

LENGTH OF WALK: 4 miles – stride it in an hour, saunter it in two.

CONDITIONS: Lanes to and from river can be very muddy.

GEAR: Waterproof footwear; binoculars and bird book for the Severn

REFRESHMENTS: White Hart, Littleton-on-Severn (0454 412275) – good hot food, good cool beer, welcoming children's room

ACCOMMODATION: Elberton Court Farm, Elberton, Nr Olveston, Thornbury, Bristol, Avon (0454 413256) – Mrs Bamfield

Poet's Corner

EDWARD THOMAS FELLOWSHIP BIRTHDAY WALK, STEEP, HAMPSHIRE

A member of the Edward Thomas Fellowship celebrating the
Birthday Walk

Driving down under the beeches into the Hampshire village of Steep, the road lay in Sunday morning emptiness. I thought I must have missed them; but there they were at the turn of the lane, striding towards me a hundred strong, walking sticks and boots clattering on the tarmac, like an earnest and kindly invading army.

The Edward Thomas Fellowship is aptly named. Good fellowship was the keynote of the day, the miles of clay slides in the beech hangers and flinty tracks along the downland ridges beguiled by friendly conversations struck up with perfect strangers. Yet fellowship is just about the last word that springs to mind when thinking of the poet and prose writer Edward Thomas. This was a man who hungered above all else for solitude, relieving his black depressions and bitter despair by wandering alone for thirty miles or more a day over the hills of his beloved South Country.

Many times during this convivial walk I found myself wondering what Thomas's reaction would have been, could he have seen our straggling company of enthusiasts gathered from all parts of Britain to celebrate his birthday, cheerfully tramping his favourite walks while quoting and reading aloud his work. Very likely he would have turned his back and marched rapidly in the opposite direction.

The Fellowship was in a collective good mood, born of the beautiful downland countryside around Steep, the mild March sunshine and the knowledge that this year's Birthday Walk had fallen on Thomas's birthday itself, 3 March. At each stile a long queue formed, old friends exchanging gossip and newer members establishing their credentials with apposite quotes. An elderly lady in a waxed coat waited patiently as a much more elderly gentleman in knee-breeches was manhandled across.

> . . . I wait his flight.
> He goes: I follow; no release
> Until he ceases,

she murmured, smiling sideways at me. I was too dull to bat back anything cleverer than an answering grin.

Edward Thomas moved with his young family to Steep in 1906, hammering out a thin living as a literary reviewer and prose writer of articles and books, few of which he had the leisure or financial security to craft as he would have wished. But this rolling, wooded countryside of chalk downs, steep slopes, tree-hung edges and far views sustained a spirit often crushed under feelings of hopelessness.

Our disjointed snake of walkers contracted again at another stile, then elongated to climb a steep path among the beeches and ancient yews of Wheatham Hill, a narrow track slippery with last autumn's sodden leaves and this wet winter's thick, adhesive white clay. With scarlet cheeks and steaming breath we topped out on the ridge of the hillside known as the Shoulder of Mutton, our reward the view between bare branches down the escarpment and away over the roofs of Steep to the tree-covered swell of the South Downs rising half a dozen miles away.

Up here on the ridge the trees had been devastated by the previous year's February gales. Scores were still lying where they had fallen, the circular white discs of their clay-matted roots in the air. The Fellowship – now well strung out and already beginning to lose a trickle of stragglers – squidged and skidded along the hill track, in and out of sunlit patches, under and over smooth grey beech trunks toppled across the path.

At intervals the Fellows had placed Edward Thomas's poems on sticks, facing the particular corners and pieces of countryside that had inspired them. At Wyke Green we halted on the road to hear a reading of 'The Path':

> The path, winding like silver, trickles on,
> Bordered and even invaded by thinnest moss
> That tries to cover roots and crumbling chalk
> With gold, olive and emerald, but in vain . . .

How clearly Thomas caught the look and the detail of those beechwood paths. The Fellows gathered round the reader, many with heads lowered, eyes closed and expressions inward and absorbed as if in prayer.

It was only in the last three years of his life, prompted by the American poet Robert Frost, that Edward Thomas began to write poetry. His prose writing had always hummed with its own poetical rhythms: 'a group of trees, a single field, a pure pool of sedge and bright water, an arm of sea, a train of clouds, a road'. But now his talent burst out in full flower, focused on this South Country and its echoes, dark and light, in his own spirit.

His first poem, 'Up in the Wind', was written about the remote pub into which the Fellowship crowded at lunchtime:

> . . . 'The White Horse' in this clump of beeches.
> It hides from either road, a field's breadth back . . .

The pub has changed very little in appearance from the turn of the century when Edward Thomas drank his ale and chatted with the farm workers in its bar – a wood-carved portrait of him hangs there now. All inside is dark, smoke-pickled, uneven and creaky. Members of the Thomas clan were gathered here, to the open delight of the Fellows – Edward's daughter Myfanwy, eighty years old, sitting bespectacled and erect in one dark corner while Birthday Walkers approached to be blessed with a handshake; the poet's nephew Edward holding unobtrusive court at a table in the sunshine outside; the poet's niece Cicely in walking boots.

After lunch, having shed a few more of our number, we moved off again over the high fields into a brisk wind. Talk among the walkers had eased down a notch or two from the high-mindedness of the morning. The donnish-looking pair ahead had their heads nodding together in solemn fashion, but the wisps of conversation blown back to me were of the plumbing-in of shower units.

A new companion was at my elbow, describing his trip to France to visit Edward Thomas's grave at Agny. The poet was killed by shell blast on the first day of the Battle of Arras at Easter 1917, aged thirty-eight. 'There was a beautiful cherry tree growing over his grave,' mused my friend, too modest to draw attention to his own poem about the visit, printed in the Fellowship newsletter as I afterwards discovered.

Half-way down the precipitous Shoulder of Mutton we halted at the Edward Thomas Memorial Stone for a final reading. Down this slope, in his sunnier moods, Edward would canter home to Berryfield Cottage below, with the infant Myfanwy shrieking on his shoulder and a breathtaking view spread out in front of him to a distant downland skyline:

> A hollow land as vast as heaven . . .
> That is how I should make hills had I to show
> One who would never see them what hills were like . . .
> Sixty miles of South Downs at one glance.
> Sometimes a man feels proud of them, as if
> He had just created them with one mighty thought.

FACT FILE

MAP: OS 1:50,000 Landranger Sheet 197 'Chichester and The Downs'

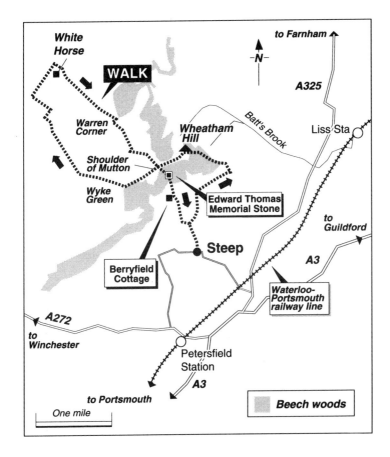

TRAVEL: To Petersfield – A3 from north and south, A272 from east and west.
Steep is 1½ miles north of Petersfield by signposted minor roads.
Park in village street near church.
Nearest railway station: Petersfield (1½ miles)

WALK DIRECTIONS: Through gate opposite Steep church (745253), across
Steep Common and through trees, bearing left around edge of Northfield
Wood to road (742258). Bear right past The Mill Water along lane for 1½
miles, passing entrance to Ashford Lane (746267), to footpath fingerpost and
stile in hedge on left (751269). Climb slope, cross stile, turn right for 15 yards,

then sharp left (750271) up steep, slippery track to trig pillar at top of Wheatham Hill (745272).

Continue along bridleway through trees to reach Wyke Green (729267). Bear right, then next left, over crossroads and on for ½ mile to turn right over stile (719268) and cut across field to Blackmore Farm. Bear right up bending lane to T-junction (712279); turn right, then left at next T-junction (714282) and right at following crossroads (709283). Go straight over main road (note blank frame of inn sign) and bear right at stile (713290) to cross field to White Horse pub (714290).

From pub take footpath in field across drive, continuing for 1½ miles to Warren Corner (727280), turning right and in 200 yards left at footpath sign, through gate and along bridleway, bearing right round wood to road (730274). Turn right, then in 50 yards left into Old Litten Lane for ½ mile to rough Cockshot Lane (737270); left here for 75 yards, then right at Hangers Way sign. Descend steep slope of Shoulder of Mutton, past Memorial Stone (739267) and over road to return to The Mill Water and Steep.

LENGTH OF WALK: 10 miles – 5 hours

CONDITIONS: Chalk tracks slippery after rain, always muddy. Steep climb up Wheatham Hill; steep descent of Shoulder of Mutton.

GEAR: Strong, waterproof footwear; splashproof or unwreckable legwear. A walking stick is handy on the steep sections.

REFRESHMENTS: White Horse, Priors Dean

ACCOMMODATION: Cricketers Inn, Steep (0730 61035)

FURTHER READING: *The Collected Poems of Edward Thomas,* (OUP paperback, 1981)
The South Country by Edward Thomas, (Dent, Everyman paperback, 1984)

FURTHER INFORMATION: The Edward Thomas Fellowship, c/o Richard Emeny, 3 South Court, Halswell House, Goathurst, Bridgwater, Somerset TA5 2DH (0278 662856)

The High and the Mighty

HIGH FORCE AND CAULDRON SNOUT, UPPER TEESDALE

The River Tees tumbles in full flood down to the craggy cleft of
High Force waterfall

'Well, what did you expect at this time of year?' snapped the sharp-nosed woman at the foot of High Force, unfolding her umbrella with a furious shake. Her husband wiped the rain and spray off his glasses, took a long and angry look at her grimly set mouth and bit back on his next complaint. He stared sulkily up at the falling water, sighing as meaningfully as he dared.

I climbed down the slippery rocks away from their squabble, giving private thanks for the cloudburst that had swept up to blanket the hills of the Durham and Cumbria border. It was the culmination of a week's bad weather that had swollen the River Tees and was now sending it crashing down the craggy amphitheatre of High Force in full and majestic flood. The water leaped downwards in yellow plumes, thundering from step to step of the dolerite staircase to plunge into a peat-brown pool at the foot of the fall. Spray drifted away like bonfire smoke, wreathing up among the green leaf buds of the trees. In such times of spate, High Force fully lives up to its reputation as the most spectacular waterfall in England.

Half a mile below the fall I crossed the Tees on a rickety bridge and headed west along the Pennine Way, savouring fond memories. Fifteen years ago I had walked here with my father, our first taste of these wild Pennine hills and peat moors. I grinned to myself as the rain beat into my face, remembering our night's stop in a dour little pub at Middleton-in-Teesdale a few miles downriver where my father had been offered a rub-down by a twenty-stone lady from Birmingham. No such adventures today – just the damp clouds on the hilltops, the sodden sheep giving me their customary indignant stare, and the prospect of fifteen miles in the company of the beautiful Tees.

The Pennine Way curved ahead, a glistening highway of peaty mud beaten out by the boots of decades of long-distance walkers. There was an exciting view of the agitated head of High Force tossing between its rock pinnacles before leaping seventy feet into space; then the broad back of the Tees winding away into a remote valley. The liquid cries of curlews came from the clouds overhead, and down on the soft ground by the river the lapwings were strutting about in pairs.

Lonely farmsteads were scattered across the wet green hillsides, the houses and barns joined together in low-standing blocks, all whitewashed. Local legend-spinners, not unwilling to make a fool out of their landlord, offer an explanation of why all the farms on the Raby Estate are painted white. The story has a former Lord Barnard arriving late one night at a dilapidated Teesdale farm in search of a bed. The nobleman, appalled that one of his properties could have got so far out of hand, declares that he will repair the farm in payment for his lodging, a deal willingly agreed by the farmer. Upon receipt of an enormous bill, the benefactor realizes that his generous offer has been made to someone else's tenant, and promptly orders all his farms painted white to avoid future cases of mistaken identity.

At Cronkley Bridge I recrossed the Tees and trudged by Langdon Beck, a bubbling stream seething round flat boulders. Widdybank Farm lay tucked down in the shelter of a shoulder of ground at the entrance to Holmwath, a wild valley devoid of roads and houses. Now the setting changed and foreshortened from open country to a steep-sided canyon above which reared grey teeth of basalt. Among the boulders at the feet of these crags I slipped and fell, bashing my elbow and knocking all the breath from my body.

What dry aside would Alfred Wainwright, that crotchety maker of handwritten guide books for walkers, have found for my pratfall? Wainwright died in January 1991 aged eighty-four, but his spirit hovers over these hills as much as it does over his beloved Lakeland. On that long-ago trek with my father we had never failed to enjoy the steely one-liners at the foot of each page of Wainwright's *Pennine Way Companion*, summing up walking conditions. 'Penance for sins' was one of our favourites; 'You will question your own sanity' was another. Now, bruised and breathless under Falcon Clints, I hauled the battered little book out of my pocket and found the Holmwath page. 'Very good' was the comment of the Master. Hmmm!

Sunshine was shredding the clouds away from the hills as I picked my way gingerly on under the crags. The Tees, as dull as sheet metal up till now, began to glint and sparkle among its rocks. The drystone walls and solitary barns high on the fellsides glowed green and gold. There was a muffled roar from up ahead, growing louder. Suddenly the rock wall gave way, and there in a narrow side valley spouted another tremendous waterfall, more racing and tumbling water crammed into a tall cleft. The vapour from the bottom pool threw a miniature rainbow into the air.

I scrambled up the rock ledges at the side, showered with spray and sheer exhilaration. 'A torrent of angry cascading waves, white with rage,' said Wainwright of Cauldron Snout. The waves of the fall were creamy-yellow today, but otherwise the old man had caught it to perfection.

At the top of Cauldron Snout another waterfall came into sight – a manmade one. Writing in the 1960s, Wainwright had deplored the scheme then being mooted to build a reservoir up here in the hills. Cow Green, the valley that lies above Cauldron Snout, was one of the rarest jewels in the botanical treasure chest of Upper Teesdale, where arctic and alpine plants like the celestially blue spring gentian, the Teesdale violet and the delicate pink birdseye primrose have survived since the end of the last Ice Age. A natural exhibition of the development of plants over 10,000 years was laid out up the slopes of Cow Green.

But the chemical industries of Teesside, thirty miles away, needed ten billion gallons of water, Conservation had no clout in those days. Cow Green was flooded, in the face of bitter protest. Today the waters of the Tees slip in graceful, slow-moving curtains down the concrete face of the reservoir dam, before exploding in frustrated power over Cauldron Snout – a poignant contrast.

The sun turned on a belated performance, burning hot on my back as I walked up the reservoir road, though there was a rising wind stiff enough to whip the water into white horses that raced on to the pebbly beaches. The Teesdale farms lay in the warm afternoon sunlight, their walls still scabbed with the winter's storm blasting, not yet smartened into another summer's whiteness. By New House, Wat Garth, Hill End and Force Garth I wandered the four miles back to High Force, tired and thirsty, nursing my aching elbow, slowly drying off and full of the sights and sounds of water and hills.

Sinking into stiffness in the lounge of the High Force Hotel, with the rumble of the fall coming faintly in through the open window, I raised a teacup to the Master. Very good, indeed.

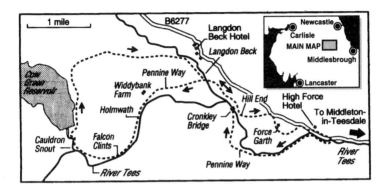

FACT FILE

MAP: OS 1:50,000 Landranger Sheet 92 'Barnard Castle and Richmond'

TRAVEL: M6 to Jct 38; A685 to Brough; B6276 to Middleton-in-Teesdale; B6277 to High Force. Park car at High Force Hotel.

WALK DIRECTIONS: From High Force (880286), right down B6277 for ⅓ mile to track on right (890284) marked 'Private road – no access for vehicles'. Cross Tees, turn right on Pennine Way for 3 miles to cross Cronkley Bridge (862293). In 1 mile cross Langdon Beck (854302) to reach Widdybank Farm (837298). Up Holmwath valley to Cauldron Snout (814287). Up right of fall to reservoir road; 1½ miles to gate (818309); right along road, and right again (832311). Cross bridge (847310); bear right immediately across fields through gates to Pennine Way at bridge (854302). Keep on left of Langdon Beck to Cronkley Bridge (862293); join farm track to Hill End (864292). Cross fields to farm track (866290) and follow to Force Garth (876287) and lane to B6277 road (881288) and High Force Hotel (885286).

LENGTH OF WALK: 15 miles – 7 hours

CONDITIONS: Rough, stony moorland walking on well-marked Pennine Way – difficult section of boulders in Holmwath – steep scramble beside Cauldron Snout – farm tracks and roads. A long and tiring walk, suitable for active walkers; in mist or heavy rain, only for the experienced.

GEAR: Proper fell-walking boots and clothing; map and compass; flower book

REFRESHMENTS: Langdon Beck Hotel (852312); High Force Hotel

ACCOMMODATION: High Force Hotel (0833 22222/22264)

FURTHER READING: *Pennine Way Companion* by A. Wainwright (pub. Westmorland Gazette)

Blue Ridge Mountains of the Costa

MIJAS, COSTA DEL SOL, SPAIN

Looking towards Mijas from the Ermita San Anton

The towering blocks of hotels and flats in Fuengirola glittered in the heat of a June morning. From Málaga to Algeciras a grey blanket of cloud was pressing down on the Costa del Sol, making a dry oven of promenades and beaches. Where to walk, away from the crowds and the dusty pavements?

Those pale blue ridges behind southern Spain's baking holiday strip, so seldom visited by the holidaymakers, held the promise of a breeze to cool a morning's ramble. My companion, seventy-six years old and spry enough, was game for a couple of not too strenuous hours. 'Try Mijas,' advised Nicola, the hardworking holiday representative at the Hotel las Palmeras in Fuengirola. 'It's a pretty village, and you'll find some nice paths into the countryside. The wild boars are only dangerous if they're hungry, so the locals tell me.'

We saw no wild boars that morning. But the long wait in the tourist office of the town hall at Mijas ('Mee-has'), where we had hoped to get information on local footpaths, was enough to make anyone snort and bare their tusks. The only maps available were those produced for car-bound tourists, useless for the would-be rambler off the beaten track. We sat cooling our heels for an hour and a half while municipal functionaries came and went, then decided to strike out for ourselves.

A wise decision, as it turned out. There were enough cramped side streets and winding alleyways in Mijas to catch the flavour of what this part of Spain must have been like thirty years ago when tourism was less important to the local economy than last night's catch of fish or today's goat-milking. But now tall cranes were swinging building materials into place on the hill-tops all around the village, busy with the transformation of this once poverty-stricken range of hills into a modern holiday paradise.

We turned off the main Fuengirola highway to follow the twisting road towards Benalmádena. Pine-covered mountains climbed away behind Mijas, their peaks shimmering in heat haze, while down towards the coast a wide view opened up over dusty, bare foothills of dry rock and scrub. Beyond these, a couple of miles south, sprawled the Costa del Sol's built-up strip of tower blocks, bars and discos, fifteen miles of holiday development now mercifully remote. Up here at the feet of the mountains the breeze was strong enough to ward off the full heat of the sun as it began to burn its way through the clouds.

A mile along the Benalmádena road the slim arches of a stone aqueduct spanned a gully, dry at this season, but during winter rains a cascade of white water leaping down to the sea. Just beyond the gully a side road marked 'Ermita San Anton' ran away and down the hillside. The tarmac petered out a few hundred yards along, where the *ermita* stood – a whitewashed little chapel, built by a local sailor in fulfilment of his side of a frantic bargain struck with the Almighty during a shipwreck.

The chapel was locked, but at the back we found a rocky

hillside where statues and memorials had been set in the parched earth. Local people evidently value their pets as much as their human relations. One much-lamented poodle had his own shrine complete with wooden kennel, a ceramic plaque bearing his portrait, and an effusive funerary ode, entitled 'La Oracian del Perro', inscribed on a large slab of marble.

Disregarding the twentieth-century monstrosities gobbling up the coastline, the view from the edge of the memorial ground was straight from a Renaissance painting. Tall, dark spikes of cypress trees stood up like lines of needles along roads too far off to be seen. The drab brown of thirty scorched hillsides rose in terraces, each level banked by curving stone buttresses, to the white walls and orange-tiled roofs of a single farmhouse or tiny hamlet perched on each flattened top. The small, baked hills were separated by dry stream gullies choked with rocks. Across the nearest valley the houses of Mijas lay in rectangular slabs of white under their steeply climbing mountainside.

My companion was content to potter among the bizarre memorial statues, but a dusty track beside the chapel beckoned me to a steep descent into one of those hot, secluded valleys. Fixing a rendezvous in an hour's time, I made off along the path which wound down the face of a cliff and wriggled its way between small fields thick with wild flowers. Furry stalks and fleshy, water-retaining leaves abounded, vital for survival in ground starved of water for most of the year.

Thumbing through my book on Mediterranean flowers, I struggled for many minutes to find the hairy leaves and pale yellow dandelion flowers of something that probably wasn't *Andryala integrifolia*. But I made pretty sure of the century plant, whose ten-foot stems leaned out from the dry earth all along the path. The Mexicans make their national drink, 'pulque', from the juice of this plant's flower spikes, according to my flower book. A cold flask of pulque would have come in handy on that exposed track, which snaked around the naked rock bluffs until it dived into the cool shade of olive trees.

Here I pulled out my Spanish phrase book and baffled an old lady with my badly pronounced enquiry about the route: 'Torreblanca, por fa-bor, ko-mo se lye-ga a-ee?' Her house was built into an overhang of rock above the path, its terrace shaded by vine leaves. 'Torreblanca!' she shouted cheerfully, pointing down the hillside while her dog growled at my dusty shoes, Torreblanca, a suburb of Fuengirola, lay out of sight a couple of miles away below a range of low, barren hillocks flayed into a waterless desert by the sun.

With my companion waiting for me in the sun up at the Ermita San Anton, the complete walk to Torreblanca was out of the question. Instead I gave myself half an hour more on the downward slope, slipping in and out of the gnarled old olive trees as the track dwindled to a narrow path under hanging faces of rock. Groves of orange trees clung to the hillsides below the path, the half-ripe fruit glowing temptingly among the leaves. Round each precipitous corner stood a farmhouse at the head of a dry valley, chicken cluckings coming drowsily from tiny walled yards in dark pools of shadow cast by fig trees.

In a dappled net of shade thrown across the path by motionless leaves I stopped to listen. Down on the coast the disco bars were packed and yelling; but up here, caught in this indigo mesh of coolness, I could hear only the farmyard chickens, the hum of insects and trickle of hidden water under the olives. Otherwise, not a sound in the still heat of midday.

FACT FILE

MAP: Spanish Ordnance Survey maps are not on sale locally – they seem to be reserved for the military. Maps available are of the tourist kind, with no footpaths marked. On this short walk you can well do without one; but if you prefer to walk with a map, bring your own to Spain with you – Spanish Ordnance Survey 1:50,000 sheet 16/45, reference name 'Coin', available from Edward Stanford Ltd., 12/14 Long Acre, Covent Garden, London WC2E 9LP.

TRAVEL: Mijas lies about 3 miles due north of Fuengirola – buses from Fuengirola bus station every half hour or so throughout the day and early evening.

WALK DIRECTIONS: From Mijas (535512) take Fuengirola road to first big right-hand bend as you leave village; Benalmádena road forks left here (541519). In about ½ mile, turn off right down track signposted 'Ermita San Anton' (548521). The track towards Torreblanca starts on left of chapel

(549519), unsignposted but clear on the ground all the way. Frequent coast buses back from Torreblanca to Fuengirola.

LENGTH OF WALK: Mijas to Torreblanca about 5 miles – 2 hours

CONDITIONS: An easy stroll, though mountain path is stony and dusty. Take plenty of sun cream and a sun hat if you intend to do the walk in the hottest months, July and August. There is a cool breeze in the mountains, but the sun can be deceptively hot. Late May and June are the best months for walking; the flowers are out, and the sun is not as fierce as it becomes later.

GEAR: Sun hat, sun cream, drinks. Flower book: *Flowers of the Mediterranean* by Oleg Polunin and Anthony Huxley (Chatto & Windus, 1981). Spanish phrase book: *Spanish* (Collins Traveller, 1990).

REFRESHMENTS: Plenty of cafés and bars in Mijas and Torreblanca – houses along the way are delighted to offer drinks, chat and advice.

INFORMATION: Mijas Town Hall is in the main square – prepare for a long wait if you are after local information, as few of the officials speak fluent English and they are apt to disappear from their offices without explanation!

FURTHER READING: For local flavour read *Blue Guide to Spain* (Benn Publications); *Southern Spain* by Elizabeth de Stroumillo (Thornton Cox, 1990).

FURTHER INFORMATION: Spanish Tourist Board: (071 499 3257); Tourist Information Office, Plaza de España, Fuengirola: (010 34 52 479500)

Still Intact, Seventy Years On

GEORGEHAM AND BRAUNTON BURROWS, DEVON

Williamson's world: the coast near Braunton

The owl stared impassively out from the dark slate gravestone on which it was carved. 'Here Rests Henry Williamson, 1895–1977' read the simple inscription. If any spot in North Devon is truly peaceful on a warm summer afternoon it is this sunlit corner of the graveyard at Georgeham, that looks through trees arching over a trickling stream to the little thatched Skirr Cottage, where the war-shocked and alienated Henry Williamson came to live in 1921.

The little village of Georgeham has a high road threaded by steady holiday traffic. But down below the church the narrow lanes with their higgledy-piggledy cottages still hold something of the peace that helped to soften the psychological agony Williamson had undergone in the Flanders trenches. Everywhere he turned there was material – human and animal – for the stories he was already beginning to write.

At that time, too, very few outsiders came to these valleys north-west of Barnstaple. There was a wild and unfrequented Atlantic coast to explore, and all of Exmoor and the North Devon cliffs and hills with their red deer, falcons and otters within a day's walk. Williamson had seven years in the deep obscurity of Georgeham, learning to write and to observe and record nature, before he found fame in 1928 with *Tarka the Otter*. Thereafter the world beat an ever-widening path to his door, finding a man who could be by turns either charming, funny and welcoming, or crotchety and abruptly dismissive.

Those early writings, usually sold for a few pounds to newspaper editors in order to pay the rent, marvellously evoke that vanished rural North Devon of the 1920s – its clannish fishing villages, its inward-looking people, its old-fashioned deer and otter hunts, its wonderful variety of wildlife in rivers, hedgerows, woods and fields. The real marvel, though, is how much of Williamson's Devon is still intact seventy years on.

As a schoolboy I discovered Henry Williamson's collection of hunting stories, *The Old Stag*, and read everything else of his I could get my hands on. Through Williamson's writing I knew intimately the sights, sounds and smells of a countryside I had never visited. That spell has never weakened: I still see North Devon through Williamson eyes, today and always.

From Skirr Cottage in Georgeham I set out to retrace one of his favourite walks, over the hill to Braunton Burrows and the estuary of the Two Rivers, and found things almost exactly as he had described them in his short story 'The Crake' from *Tales of Moorland and Estuary*.

In the hamlet of Forda, a mile along the B3231 road, I found the lane which Williamson often climbed, 'a steep and narrow lane, or rather gulley, for its stony bed was a-trickle with water, as one entered a dark tunnel under blackthorn bushes'. The tall hedges under the wind-stunted blackthorns were choked with a dense mass of pink campion, purple foxgloves, yellow buttercups and goatsbeard, long green hart's-tongue ferns lapping up the water running down the stony margins of the lane. It looked as if no one had come this way all summer, for the flowers and grasses from each hedge had met and tangled in the middle, leaving the narrowest of paths up which I sweated to the crest of the hill.

'It was a steady pull up the lane,' noted Williamson, 'but at the top there was bright reward. I stood in the clear air of morning gazing over hundreds of square miles of land and sea.' After the steep climb I was glad to stop, lean on a gate and gaze my fill round the horizon at the breathtaking view, one of the finest and furthest-flung in the West Country.

In front and to the south the two great rivers of Taw and Torridge joined forces to sweep out over Bideford Bar into the Atlantic, while inland the thick, sinuous arm of the Taw narrowed as it burrowed under red and green hills towards the many-arched bridge at Barnstaple. Further in the distance rose the beacons of Exmoor, hazed into pale blue on this first properly hot day of summer.

At my feet spread Braunton Burrows, a round-nosed promontory of scrub-covered sand dunes between estuary and open sea. The lane dropped sharply from the hill to wind as a faintly marked path for four lonely and soft-footed miles across the hollow backs of the dunes, where tall blue spikes of viper's bugloss stood among the waving quills of marram grass. A pair of lovers lay entwined among the sandhills, but there was no one else to enjoy the lark song pouring from a brassy sky over the Burrows, in whose oasis Henry Williamson often wandered to ease his darkened spirit.

Down at Crow Point on the curved tail of Braunton Burrows a skeleton lighthouse warns ships off the treacherous sandbanks. Here Williamson would stand, holding his shoes in one hand and waving a handkerchief in the other to attract the attention of the fishermen lounging on the quay across the estuary in Appledore village. One of them would be sure to come over to Crow Point, to earn a shilling by rowing the young writer back to the Royal George by the slipway in Appledore for a lunch of bread, cheese and beer.

There was no sign of activity today, though, among Appledore's colour-washed Georgian sea-captains' houses under their round green hill. I didn't particularly want to ride over the estuary, in any case. There were five straight miles of butter-yellow firm sand to walk, back up the seaward edge of the Burrows to Saunton village under Saunton Down.

I crunched along over a carpet of flat, sun-warmed pebbles and blue mussel shells on the tideline, where Williamson recorded finding skeletons of birds struck down by the peregrine falcons that nested in the cliffs of his uncrowded, unpolluted Devon. The few holidaymakers basting themselves on the griddle of the sands this oven-hot morning didn't bother to turn their red faces to watch me walk by. The car park at Saunton was half full, but nobody drove down the short stretch of B3231 that returned me to the foot of the flowery lane. In perfect solitude I retraced my steps over the ridge and back to Georgeham.

At Ox's Cross on top of the hill, a mile north of the village, Henry Williamson's wooden hut stands among trees facing a superb view over the Two Rivers estuary and the Devon hills. In this little building is a modest collection of items personal to the writer: a few pairs of shoes and boots, his spectacles on the table, his old checked jacket across a chair-back, a photograph of him as a young man at the height of his *Tarka* fame. Williamson lived and worked in the hut for months at a time over many years, finding here the silence and freedom he always craved.

In the Rock Inn at Georgeham was another photograph of Henry Williamson, raising a glass with the landlord. It was probably those early North Devon years that brought him the most lasting peace he knew in a long, lonely and often unhappy life, blighted by dreadful wartime experiences as a young man. I sipped a welcome pint and opened *Tales of Moorland and Estuary* to read his summing-up of the morning's glorious walk: 'a timeless walk, every moment lived in peace; a walk that seems to go on for ever, and then it is all behind one, but living in the mind, timelessly.'

FACT FILE

MAP: OS 1:50,000 Landranger Sheet 180 'Barnstaple and Ilfracombe'

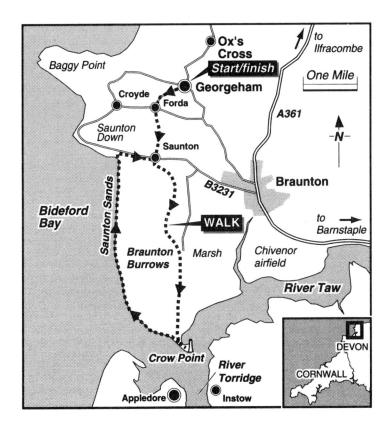

TRAVEL: A361 to Barnstaple and Braunton; B3231 to Croyde and Georgeham

Nearest railway station – Barnstaple

WALK DIRECTIONS: From Georgeham, take B3231 south for 1 mile to Forda; turn left (457391) for 100 yards to pass South Hole Farm gateway. 50 yards along lane (458390) public footpath sign points to right up hill track.

In 1 mile cross B3231 (458376); 'Coast Path' sign points to 4-mile path south over Braunton Burrows. Reach estuary at Crow Point (466318); turn right to walk 5 miles north along Saunton Sands to car park (445377). 100 yards up lane, 'Coast Path' sign points through bracken for ½ mile to rejoin

B3231. Lane back to Forda and Georgeham is 300 yards along on left. Ox's Cross is 1 mile north of village (470407).

LENGTH OF WALK: 13 miles – 5 hours

CONDITIONS: Hill lane jungly, otherwise straightforward
NB Braunton Burrows are occasionally used for military training exercises (red warning flags), but walk route keeps clear.

GEAR: Good walking shoes, trousers against prickles in lane, binoculars

REFRESHMENTS AND ACCOMMODATION: The Rock Inn, Georgeham (0271 890322)

FURTHER READING: 'The Crake' in *Tales of Moorland and Estuary* by Henry Williamson (Macdonald Futura)
Tales of a Devon Village by Henry Williamson (Faber)
Henry Williamson – A Portrait by Daniel Farson (Robinson Publishing)

Bog Dogs and Irishmen

BANGOR TRAIL, NEPHIN BEG MOUNTAINS, COUNTY MAYO, IRELAND

Oliver Geraghty was a cheerful companion, making light of the
weary miles

Boots in one hand and socks in the other, I stepped gingerly into the ice-cold waters of the Tarsoghaunmore River, saying something short and sharp to myself. Oliver Geraghty waited patiently on the far bank, watching my midstream flounderings with amusement. 'The fellow I was with last time,' commented Oliver, smiling from ear to ear, 'he slipped and went right in, with his boots round his neck. We had a good laugh about that one.'

The Bangor Trail is the loneliest hill track in Ireland, twenty-eight rugged miles through the heart of the Nephin Beg mountains in north-west County Mayo. Today the Nephin Beg had veiled their shining quartzite peaks in mist, and six miles into the trail I had yet to see further than the nearest heathery slope. But with Oliver by my side I faced the hills with confidence.

Oliver Geraghty is a rather remarkable person. Most young people emigrate from Mayo when they leave school, for the jobs and bright lights of Dublin, Birmingham or Chicago. But Oliver has stayed on, to teach others the outdoor skills he's learned. He is a canoeist and rock-climber, a mountain leader and long-distance runner and marathon cyclist.

He was a cheerful companion on the Bangor Trail, too, beguiling the weary miles with tall stories of ravening Bog Dogs and other unlikely hazards of the hill. Best of all, he never faltered when the trail disappeared, as it did on more than one occasion.

Oliver and I had made good time coming south from Bangor Erris, the little one-street town at the northern end of the trail. Now, with the Tarsoghaunmore River behind us, we set our boots to the hillside in earnest, climbing up into the mist over the steep shoulder of Nephin Beg Mountain. This is wild walking. There are no waymarks, no bridges, no handy signposts – just the faint line of the track running ahead.

The old road has deteriorated a long way since cattle drovers and hardy travellers tramped it through the Nephin Beg. For centuries it was the only route into the remote boglands round Bangor Erris. But these days the track is rarely walked.

Parts are knee-deep in sinking bog; other stretches have vanished under grass, stones and heather. The loneliest parts of England's now boot-battered Pennine Way, in its early years of obscurity, were like this; map-and-compass country, where an unwary walker can easily go astray many miles from help.

In the nethermost depths of the Nephin Beg lies the great bog-filled saucer of Scardaun Valley, utterly silent, five miles at least from any house or road. The Bangor Trail (at its half-way point here) ribbons along the hill slopes above the flat floor of the valley. In its carpet of wet brown bog lie the green outlines of ancient 'lazybeds', the heaped ridges of seaweed and manure in which crops were once laboriously grown.

The potatoes of Scardaun, like those of the rest of Ireland, rotted into black slime in the lazybeds during the Great Famine of 1845–9. This part of County Mayo lost a quarter of its people to death or emigration.

Along the valley the trail is dotted with roofless shells of abandoned stone cabins where children were raised by the dozen. Oliver and I rested in the shadow of one, nibbling chocolate and cupping our hands in a little waterfall for mouthfuls of cold, peaty water.

In his book *Sketches in Erris and Tyrawley*, published in 1839, the Revd Caesar Otway describes the meal of potatoes and home-distilled whiskey he was given at a house in Scardaun. He spent an uncomfortable and draughty night on the floor there, with his host's entire family lying on guard between him and the eldest daughter. The clergyman had not enjoyed his ride along 'the old and only pass into Erris . . . Who would venture on its unpleasant ways but the smuggler or the outlaw?'

Suddenly the mist lifted as we sat there by the tumbledown house, baring the craggy back of Glennamong Mountain dead ahead and printing high peaks and ridges on the clouds all round. The roadless lost valley lay revealed for a minute or two as the hub of a spectacular circle of mountain heights. Then the mist swirled across again, reimposing the narrow limits of bog, slope and line of stony trail. We sluiced our faces in the waterfall and scrambled on under Glennamong, out of the hills and into the forestry.

Tremendous blocks of conifers have been planted around the feet of the Nephin Beg, unsoftened by the discreet screens of broadleaved trees demanded by conservationists in Britain. Instead, the green and black battalions march in naked uniformity up and across the hillsides. The Altaconey River snakes over a rocky bed beneath the glowering trees. Locals call this place 'Canada', and with good reason.

Oliver led me up and over the trackless ridge of Sheep Pass, and down the forest tracks to Srahmore Lodge. Here we found Joe McDermott waiting with a grin of welcome and an outstretched hand, ready to walk the last seven miles into Newport with us.

Joe and his wife Pauline have shaken a lot of healthy life into Mayo since they moved out here from Dublin to set up the

Skerdagh outdoor recreation centre, which they run with the help of Oliver. The three of them act as sheepdogs on the annual Bangor Trail walk in June, when several score adventurers tramp the rough miles through the Nephin Beg from Newport to Bangor Erris, and then get stuck into an almighty party.

'Hill walking is not a big thing in Ireland,' Joe told me as we swung along the road towards Newport, 'People tend to think you're a bit mad if you walk for pleasure. But it's starting to happen. Still plenty of unvisited mountains in remote parts like this, though, thank God.'

It was getting towards dusk as we came down into Newport. There was freshly caught Atlantic salmon on the table at De Bille House, and dark, delicious Guinness in Frank Chambers' bar. Sitting there at an undisclosable hour, by now feeling the long trek in my feet and calves, I raised a grateful glass to Oliver Geraghty.

His grandfather, however, would probably have dismissed the pair of us as weak-kneed milksops. That hardy man regularly drove cattle from south of Newport along the 'old and only pass' to Bangor Erris market. There he would buy new beasts and walk home with them the same day: sixty-four miles in hobnail boots.

FACT FILE

MAP: Irish Ordnance Survey ½-inch Sheet 6 'North Mayo' – available from Irish Ordnance Survey Office, Phoenix Park, Dublin, Eire, or from Edward Stanford Ltd., 12/14 Long Acre, Covent Garden, London WC2E 9LP – tel 071 836 1321

TRAVEL: from north and east: N59 to Ballina, Crossmolina and Bangor Erris. From south: N60 to Castlebar, L136 to Bellacorick, N59 to Bangor Erris.

WALK DIRECTIONS: *NB Unless you are a very fit and experienced hill walker, don't try this walk on your own. Contact Joe or Pauline McDermott or Oliver Geraghty at Skerdagh Outdoor Recreation Centre (address and phone below) to arrange a companion.*

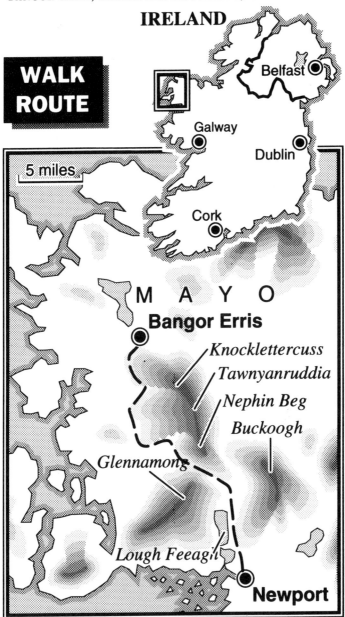

Start at Owenmore River Lodge Hostel just south of Bangor Erris (865227). Trail runs south around western flank of Knocklettercuss to reach Tarsoghaunmore River (866160). Ford river (in rare spates high enough to make it impassable, there's a footbridge ¾ mile downstream); trail all but disappears here, but bear *right* round right flank of small hill to rediscover track running north up narrow valley.

Trail climbs over shoulder of Tawnyanruddia, and follows curve of Scardaun Valley to cross Scardaun River falls (916110) under Nephin Beg Mountain. It climbs over shoulder of Nephin Beg and bears left under Glennamong Mountain to reach outskirts of forestry plantation (940072).

From here: (a) **in dry weather** continue along trail, keeping forest on your left, until trees open out after 2 miles. Follow forestry fence sharply to left to ford Altaconey River (967055) and climb stile in wire fence. Go left for 20 yards, then across grass under trees for 100 yards to turn right on forest road. Take every right turn thereafter to reach Srahmore Lodge.

(b) **in or after heavy rain** Altaconey River may be unfordable. After reaching forestry, take first gate on left into trees and keep on forest roads, taking every right turn to reach Srahmore Lodge.

From Srahmore Lodge (975043) 7 miles of road lead into Newport; or you can take first turn on left after reaching Lough Feeagh (971012) on high hill track across shoulder of Buckoogh to join road at 973980.

LENGTH OF WALK: 28 miles approx – allow at least 12 hours, with 2 good rests.

CONDITIONS: Wet, boggy, rough hill walking – a long, tiring day. Make sure someone knows where you are going.

GEAR: Full hill-walking gear and survival equipment; plenty of food; hot drink

ACCOMMODATION: Hillcrest House, Bangor Erris ((010 353) 97 83494); De Bille House, Newport ((010 353) 97 41145)

FURTHER INFORMATION: Skerdagh Outdoor Recreation Centre, Glenhest, Newport, County Mayo, Eire ((010 353) 98 41647/41500); Irish Tourist Board, 150–1 New Bond Street, London W1Y 0AQ (071 493 3201)

Warm Country with a Heart of Iron

NETTLETON BECK, LINCOLNSHIRE

Following the Nettleton Beck: 'Few visitors seek out these fastnesses,
and the local people like it that way'

There is iron in the soul of Nettleton. This Lincolnshire farming village is built of ironstone, richly golden stuff that crumbles beneath a rub of the finger and smears with rusty streaks after rain. The ironstone has been dug over the centuries from the sides of the steep valleys that cradle Nettleton in the flanks of the Lincolnshire wolds.

It's rolling country hereabouts, with an airy upland feel, quite unlike the flat fens and coastal clays and silts that one tends to associate with England's least 'discovered' county. The Lincolnshire wolds, running north and south for thirty miles, have an enclosed beauty of hidden valleys and unexpected vistas at the turn of a corner – a sweeping view over ten or fifteen miles of farmland, perhaps, or a thousand-year-old church tower rising over a tucked-away village. Few visitors seek out these fastnesses, and the local people like it that way.

A misty summer's morning was settling over Nettleton as I wandered up the street. A tractor went clattering by, shedding wisps of hay from its laden trailer, its roar soon overlain by the crowing of cocks from the farmyards and bleating of sheep on the green hillsides that filled in the gaps between the dark gold houses.

Thistles and grasses waved high over the heads of stone seraphim kneeling in the overgrown north quarter of the grave-yard. The massive tower of the church of St John the Baptist stood on a base laid down before the Norman Conquest. The tower buttresses had been nibbled and chiselled away by wind and rain over the centuries, giving the church the appearance of something quarried entire rather than built.

The Viking Way long-distance footpath winds through the village on its 112-mile journey from the River Humber to Rutland Water in Leicestershire. The horned-helmet symbols pointed me aside into the valley of the Nettleton Beck, one of those silent and sunken dingles where no other walkers ever seem to be.

The last time I came this way, four or five years ago, I had seen no one; and now, too, I trod the rough track beside the beck with only myself and the rabbits for company. They were everywhere, scurrying across the newly cut hayfields, scrabbling into burrows in the loose sandy soil and bobbing in among the meadowsweet and campion along the stream.

Stands of willows grew tall in the valley floor, nourished by streamlets running down the wet, rushy slopes. Snipe burst out from under my boots, zigzagging startlingly away with a squawk and a flash of brown and white, their tiny sickle-shaped wings whirring. A sparrowhawk darted up and over the skyline from the branch where it had been sitting on watch for small birds.

The sky thickened and darkened overhead, pressing down on the valley as it swung left and right on its climb to the crest of the wolds. Nettleton Beck, narrow enough to step over, chinked and trickled in a green tunnel of foliage. The suck of a cow's hooves came clearly through the still air as it squelched down to drink at the beck two hundred yards away. Silence lay as thickly as the air haze in the lonely valley. Yet only a few decades ago it had hummed with industry.

At the top of the slopes each side of the path the chalk showed whitely through the turf. Chalk and sand were quarried along with the ironstone for centuries here, and the scars of their diggings and delvings still pit the landscape. Chalk on top of sand; an unstable combination, which has settled and shifted over the years to form long terraces running high above the valley. In the last decades of the seventeenth century twenty-five of Nettleton's houses were smothered by sand creeping down out of the hillside. It's a landscape in motion, lumpy and undulating, in which the new conifer plantations cling like burrs in a sheep's back.

Below Nettleton Top Farm the Viking Way plunged in among the trees and lost itself in a jungle of pink-tipped rosebay willowherb. I waded through, dislodging snails with bright yellow shells, to come suddenly on the dark mouth of a tunnel that bored through an embankment built to carry a narrow-gauge railway from the ironstone mines down to the main line a few fields away.

Men from Nettleton village joined itinerant workers from further afield in the mines, driving level galleries into the hillsides or skimming off great areas of turf and chalk in sprawling opencast mines. Since the last ironstone was extracted back in 1969 the grass and trees have reclaimed the old mines, but the ground is still hummocked with their scoops and spoil mounds.

Now the valley climbed into open grassland, and I followed it up along the ever-narrowing Nettleton Beck. Under a hedgebank the stream trickled from a spring into a tiny pool, its surface quivering with long-legged insects.

There were more hollows and humps in the field above the spring, all that was left of the medieval village of Wykeham – perhaps abandoned when the Black Death struck, perhaps emptied by a changing climate and a search for easier ground. All Nettleton's land had been contained in just two enormous fields in those days, a thousand acres each, that stretched from the village for two long miles up the valley to the source of the beck. When the land was enclosed in the 1790s the villagers saw their common land hedged about and cultivated and their rents quadrupled.

Nettleton may have resented those enclosing hedges when they were first planted, but today they are invaluable havens for wildlife in the intensively farmed corn lands around Acre House Farm. The fields of Acre House are shaggy-edged with luxuriant hedges and uncultivated headlands. There are thick stands of broadleaved trees, ponds and ditches around the farm.

Curious to meet the farmer responsible for this oasis of conservation in a matt yellow plateau of grain, I knocked at the door of Acre House Farm. Five minutes later I was sitting with a glass of orange juice among tables heaped with crockery (they were in the middle of painting the house) while Motley Brant and his wife Corinne explained their philosophy.

'As few chemicals as we can get away with,' said Motley, blue paintbrush in hand, 'and as many uncut verges and hedges as we can manage. We get little owls, barn owls, finches, lots of butterflies, hares, wild flowers. It saddens me to see other farms with their fields ploughed right up to the roadside and the hedges all trimmed off short. We like to see the wildlife, that's what it is.'

Out in the farmyard the Brants' son Jonathan, also a farmer, gave enthusiastic agreement to his parents' approach. Down at Nettleton Top he's doing the same sort of thing. This year the Brants have left their roadside verges uncut for the first time. Spangled with blue, yellow and pink, they made a *via gloriosa* – scabious, vetch, yarrow, ragwort, mayweed, bindweed, knapweed – on which, as the murk began to clear during the two mile walk back to Nettleton, I looked out from the spine of the wolds over twenty misty miles of Lincolnshire.

FACT FILE

MAP: OS 1:50,000 Landranger Sheet 113 'Grimsby'

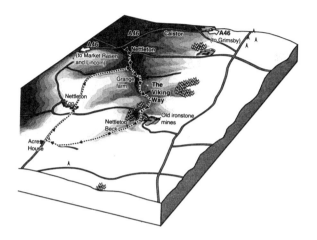

TRAVEL: From north (Humber Bridge and A15) or west (Scunthorpe and A18) – A1084 to Caistor, A46 to Nettleton. From east (Grimsby) and south (Lincoln) – A46 to Nettleton. Park by church.

Nearest railway stations: Market Rasen (8 miles) and Brigg (10 miles).

WALK DIRECTIONS: Leaving church (111002) walk east up village street; bear right round bend after 200 yards and continue for ¼ mile to fork in road just past Whitestone Cottage (113997). Bear left here at Viking Way horned-helmet symbol on to farm track to Grange Farm (116995). Keep left around edge of reservoir above farm and follow valley up, keeping Nettleton Beck on your right.

Cross paved road (122984) below Nettleton Top Farm and continue through plantation, through railway embankment tunnel and on up to stile above source of beck (120971). Follow line of telegraph poles up to cross kissing gate at top of valley on right, on to track which reaches road opposite Acre House Farm (114969). Turn right and walk along road back down to Nettleton.

LENGTH OF WALK: 5½ miles – 2 hours approx

CONDITIONS: Easy walking on roads, tracks, paths. Some muddy patches.

GEAR: Good walking shoes; flower book

REFRESHMENT: Salutation Inn, Nettleton (on A46)

ACCOMMODATION (10 miles): Mrs Curd, Hoe Hill Farm, Swinhope, Binbrook, Lincolnshire LN3 6HX (047 283 206)

FURTHER READING: *The Viking Way* (Cicerone Press)

Lights Up on the Grandest of Finales

PISTYLL RHAEADR,
CLWYD/POWYS BORDER, NORTH WALES

Pistyll Rhaeadr: 240 feet of tumbling water

The sun had only just got its head above the rounded green billows of the Berwyn Hills, and not a tractor was stirring. I drove through the sleeping village of Llanrhaeadr-ym-Mochnant ('the church by the falls of the stream where the pigs are found') and on up the winding valley road that draws a sinuous line alongside the Afon Rhaeadr between Powys and Clwyd. Four miles north-west of the village the little road gave a final wiggle and expired in the shadows at the feet of the Berwyns, cradled in the hard grey bosom of the steep-sided valley.

During those four miles I had tried my damnedest to maintain as much 'eyes-right' as was consistent with keeping the car on the road. I didn't want to spoil the unfolding drama of the sunrise walk by sneaking a premature look at the dramatic last act. But when you're facing one of the Seven Wonders of Wales before breakfast, good intentions are apt to come unstuck.

At least I managed to keep Pistyll Rhaeadr more or less in the wings. A couple of glimpses of white water tumbling behind the curtain of trees at the head of the valley, and then I was parking the car and willing myself to turn my back on the highest waterfall in Wales. I would be making my way through those trees on the far side of the valley in an hour's time, and then Pistyll Rhaeadr could burst upon me in majesty as a grand finale to the walk.

The falls were out of sight behind me now, but very far from out of earshot. Their distant splash and rumble drifted seductively on the still air of eight o'clock in the morning. They sounded a softening undertone to the harsh note of dark rock in this lonely crevice of the hills, which opened out and took on a thin coat, green of grass and brown of bracken, as I walked back down the valley.

Soon the road began to climb the hillside, looking down on the Afon Rhaeadr fifty feet below. The shallow river rushed among stunted trees in the shadows down there, snaking among gigantic square boulders lying where they had toppled through the ages from the crags overhead. The sun hauled itself up over the rim of the valley, striking out gleams from the water. On the slopes above the road the dew-soaked fleeces of the sheep were suddenly transformed in pearly splendour.

A mile down the road I turned off through the farmyard of Tyn-y-wern, where a flight of worn steps led up to an ancient stone barn. The farm cats fled, horrified at the appearance of a stranger at such an ungodly hour. I squelched down through the mud of the farm track and crossed a bridge over the Afon Rhaeadr, plunging back from bright sunshine into deepest shade.

The steep valley side rose in front of me on the southern side of the river, its flank creased by one of the narrow clefts known as a 'cwm'. In the fingers of the sunless cwm a farm lay pinched, its low-roofed, whitewashed buildings of rough stone huddled together as if for warmth.

The farmer was already astir, shouting and striding after his sheep on the hillside above the farm. The young sheepdogs he was training howled and yelped as he whistled and cursed them into line, while in the farmyard two collies that had been left behind gnawed their chains in frustration as I went by.

Now I was facing up the valley again, with evidence of long-silent industrial workings all around. Until quite recently these outposts of the Berwyn Hills were quarried for stone and mined for lead, and the greened-over quarry track I was following led me among the ruins of the old buildings. Grey screes of spoil funnelled down out of the hillside and spread in fan shapes over the lower slopes.

Ahead above the treetops I could just make out a frothy white bar where Pistyll Rhaeadr was curving over for its mighty downward leap. Across the river the spoil-scarred sides of the Nant-y-Llyn cwm slowly parted to reveal the rocky spine of 2,700-foot Moel Sych, the highest crown of the Berwyn Hills.

I walked on, with the sound of the falls growing ever louder, among boulders fallen from the sheer rock bluffs towering over me, and through a wood of silver birches, twisted old crab trees and thorn bushes red with berries. Pistyll Rhaeadr flickered white between the tree trunks, a tantalizing prelude to the final revelation.

From the footbridge over the pool at the base of the fall I gazed up at the numbing spectacle of 240 feet of furiously tumbling water. Pistyll Rhaeadr crashed down unimpeded from its upper lip in a straight fall of well over a hundred feet, thundering into a pool from which it jetted out again through a natural rock arch, seething on down into the basin at its foot.

The spray puffed and smoked out through the arch, and blasts of icy air swept round me on the footbridge. The fall

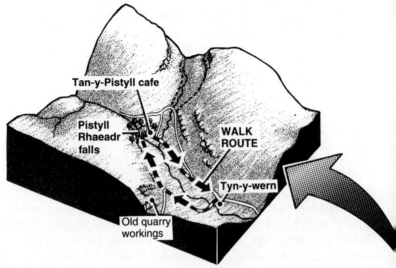

roared and hissed, shaking the rocks of its funnel with its battering force. No hellfire sermon could be more salutary than the raw power of Pistyll Rhaeadr, uplifting the spirit even as it crushes the ego of the mesmerized onlooker.

George Borrow, the indefatigable East Anglian wanderer and marvellously imperfect scholar who would have given his right arm to have been born a Welshman, came to see the fall in 1854 while he was researching his book *Wild Wales*. He thought it exceeded all the remarkable cataracts in Britain for altitude, beauty and grace – though he would have liked 'nature in one of her floods' to sweep away the 'ugly black bridge of rock' halfway up the fall. A local woman told him how she had seen a Russian visitor wriggling like an eel over the bridge.

'What shall I liken Pistyll Rhaeadr to?' mused Borrow. 'I scarcely know, unless to an immense skein of silk agitated and disturbed by tempestuous blasts, or to the long tail of a grey courser at furious speed.'

I tore myself away from the hypnotic water at last and tottered up the path back to the car, parked beside a farmhouse. George Borrow came to this house to drink buttermilk after viewing Pistyll Rhaeadr. He found a poem about the fall written in Welsh in the visitors' book, 'which though incorrect in its prosody I thought stirring and grand'. Borrow wrote out a translation which he made up on the spot:

> *Foaming and frothing from mountainous height,*
> *Roaring like thunder the Rhyadr falls;*
> *Though its silvery splendour the eye may delight,*
> *Its fury the heart of the bravest appals.*

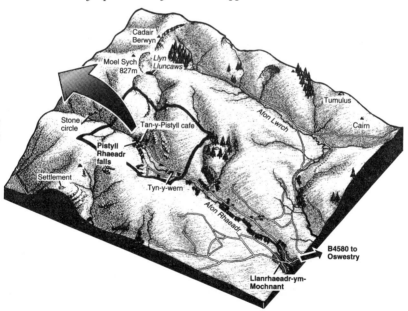

I wish I could claim to have matched him there, but my mind was fixed on something rather less profound. Bacon and eggs, to be exact.

FACT FILE

MAP: OS 1:50,000 Landranger Sheet 125 'Bala and Lake Vyrnwy'

TRAVEL: To Oswestry via A483 (from north or south); via A495 or A5 (from east). From Oswestry B4580 to Llanrhaeadr-ym-Mochnant (12 miles). Road up Afon Rhaeadr valley runs north-west from village. Park immediately below falls.

WALK DIRECTIONS: From parking place (074295) walk back along road for just over a mile, to turn right through farmyard of Tyn-y-wern (085287). Follow track down to cross river (084286); continue past farm (081285) on old quarry track which divides into 3 just beyond farm. Take middle path through ruined buildings, bearing steeply up hill at end to find clear path making straight ahead (keep fence on your right). Path is now waymarked with yellow arrows. Continue towards head of valley, making for the sound – and soon the sight – of Pistyll Rhaeadr (072295).

LENGTH OF WALK: 2½ miles – one hour

CONDITIONS: Easy family stroll, but muddy stretches near farms

GEAR: Walking shoes or gumboots; camera and plenty of film

REFRESHMENTS: Tan-y-Pistyll café beside the fall (open all weekends and school holidays; open weekdays in fine weather, Easter to end October). 3 pubs in Llanrhaeadr-ym-Mochnant: Wynnstay Arms, The Hand, Three Tuns.

ACCOMMODATION: Mrs Jean Morgan, Llys Morgan Guest House, Llanrhaeadr-ym-Mochnant, Oswestry, Salop SY10 0JZ 0691 89345

FURTHER READING: *Wild Wales* by George Borrow (Century paperback)
The Welsh Borders by Christopher Somerville, with photographs by John Heseltine (George Philip)

High Time to Go Braving the Elements

OCHIL HILLS, SCOTLAND

Bernard and Richardson: '50 miles of Scotland lay at our feet'

'As for Thursday's weather – I don't think I dare show you that just yet,' finished the TV weatherman with a meaningful smile.

You take a gamble when you plan a walk in the Scottish hills on the edge of winter. The east coast was in for a post-equinoctial battering, with cold winds set to pour down from the Arctic. Things didn't look too good that Tuesday night in Edinburgh.

Dave Richardson grimaced at me over the rim of his Macallan. He had been looking forward to giving me the annual Richardson Field Course for Wide-Eyed Amateurs on the birds and plants of the Scottish uplands. Hard man on the hill though he is, however, Dave knows which side his boots are greased.

He'd been chilled and soaked on a recent expedition, and wasn't anxious to repeat the experience.

As things turned out, we managed to slip up into the Ochils and down again before the weatherman's little hint grew teeth. But with Dick Bernard of Coalsnaughton as our guide, I think I'd have braved anything short of a full-blown gale.

No wonder Dick has never been tempted to move house. Neither would I, if I could gaze out every morning at the view that greets him when he opens his curtains. Dick lives only an hour's drive north-west of Edinburgh, but this is another world entirely. The former mining village of Coalsnaughton looks across the valley of the River Devon to the huddled mill town of Tillicoultry, and Tillicoultry looks straight up into the folded arms of the Ochil Hills.

The hills climb skyward like a wall at the back of the town, rising two thousand feet in less than a mile. They bulge and billow, their flanks cleft by narrow glens where the burns that once powered the valley mills tumble down. With the morning sun brushing their grass with creamy light, they beckoned the three of us up above the river mists like sirens.

In Tillicoultry Mill Glen the burn leapt down its staircase of rocks under birch trees thick with yellow leaves and rowans laden with scarlet berries. Dave gave me chapter and verse on the lifestyle of the black spleenwort while Dick Bernard led the way, thumping his brass-topped staff on the steps of the steep path.

Dick's back is bent with arthritis these days, legacy of sixty years' hard labour in the mill and out in all weathers maintaining the roads and railway tracks of his native Clackmannanshire. But he forged ahead like a man a third of his age, stopping every so often to run appreciative eyes across a landscape whose every inch he has explored in a long lifetime spent exclusively in Scotland.

With Tillicoultry's clattering quarry soon below us ('They shouldnae have allowed this,' muttered Dick as the stone dust clouds drifted towards the town) we crossed a bridge jammed over a dark gorge where the rotting timbers of a mill dam lay wedged. At the head of the glen the Gannel and Dalglen burns rushed together under The Law, a pointed cap of whinstone outlined against the clouds. 'Up the hillside,' said Dick, pointing aloft with his stick and crunching away over the bracken.

Before motor cars came into Clackmannanshire, mill hands from all over the district would walk ten or fifteen miles across the Ochils to their week's work in Tillicoultry, returning home at the weekend along the same lonely hill tracks. One of these overgrown high roads took us up past the fallen boulder of John Knox's Chair ('If he'd gone to preach everywhere they say he did,' Dick smiled, 'he'd not have had *time* to preach') to the rounded brow of The Pirrack, where we halted for a good stare at the view.

Fifty miles of Scotland lay spread at our feet, from the blue-grey line of the Campsie Fells near Glasgow to the sweep of the Pentlands and Muirfoots beyond Edinburgh. The broad River Forth snaked and gleamed down in the plain. 'Strange to think', ruminated Dave as he leaned on a fence post, 'that the Forth once flowed into the Rhine. Must have been a hell of a valley – there's 600 feet of sediment built up down there.'

We moved on across The Pirrack's tussocky grass to where its slope steepened and fell away into the precipitous glen of the Kirk Burn. Sitting out of the wind, sandwiches in hand and that gigantic plain in view, we were spellbound by eupepticity. I lay back in the grass, dreamily listening to bird talk.

'The nest was over yon . . . a wee bird, with a yellow beak.'

'Dunlin, would it have been? Pipit? . . . Twite?'

'You have it! A twite!'

The wide practical knowledge that Dick Bernard has amassed about his beloved Ochils has not been handed to him on a privileged plate. There were always books in the house of his father, a coal miner, but once Dick had left school to work in the mill it was self-help all the way, a gradual education of the five senses by bus, bicycle and public library.

Naturalist, explorer, photographer, historian, sound-recordist: Dick learned these trades the hard way. He read Gilbert White, Richard Jefferies and the sonnets of Shakespeare. After retirement he found out that he was a writer, too. That's how I first got to know of him, happening upon one of the paperback collections of Ochil walks he's had published by Clackmannan District Libraries.

Long before meeting Dick I'd scrambled in imagination with him up The Law and Ben Cleuch in snow, slogged through the Maddy Moss in summer and knocked at the door of the Back-hill Hoose for a mug of milk 'straucht frae the coo'. Now, lazing on The Pirrack, his talk was shot with the Doric phrases, clarity of description and glints of humour familiar to me from those plainly produced thin booklets.

Dave Richardson and I had come to the Ochils ready for anything. Judged by his writings, Dick Bernard could well have been game for a lung-racking twenty miles over heather and bog. But we'd all tacitly settled for spending our breath on amicable blether instead. Now the temperature began to drop, nipping fingers and lowering the clouds. Maybe the TV weatherman was about to redeem his credibility after all.

We shook off the crumbs for the pipits and twites, got reluctantly up and turned back over the brow of The Pirrack. 'Sand and coal – that's what this valley is made of,' remarked Dick, waving his stick over Tillicoultry like a prophet admonishing a backsliding people. 'Those new houses down there are built on sand. Most of the folk in them don't know that, of course.'

On the far side of the Mill Glen a crevice high in the hills held a few tattered pine trees, relics of the great Wood of Caledon that once clothed all these Scottish hills. A thousand feet below us, as we threaded our way down through seas of bracken on the steep breast of The Pirrack, the little towns and villages at the feet of the Ochils lay strung out along the winding course of the River Devon.

Dick smiled with pleasure as he leaned on his stick again and looked out at his home country. Eighty years of the Ochils, and still he's not seen enough of them.

FACT FILE

MAP: OS 1:50,000 Landranger Sheet 58 'Perth to Alloa'

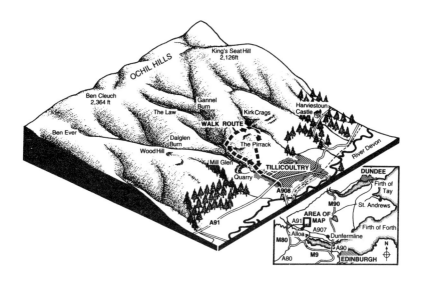

TRAVEL: From Edinburgh – A90, Forth Road Bridge, M90 to Jct 2, A823 to Dunfermline and Alloa, A908 to Tillicoultry.

From Glasgow – A80, M80, M876, A876 to Kincardine Bridge; A977, A907 to Alloa; A908 to Tillicoultry.

From Perth – A9 to Auchterarder, A823 to Yetts o' Muckhart, A91 to Dollar and Tillicoultry.

Park at bottom of Mill Glen at western edge of Tillicoultry.

WALK DIRECTIONS: From car park (914975) walk up path beside Mill Burn. After ¾ mile at head of glen where Dalglen and Gannel burns meet (912982), bear east across head of The Pirrack (marked '384 metres' on map) to look down on Kirk Craigs and the Kirk Glen (922984). A path – the Sled Road – leads down into this glen if you want to return by way of the feet of the Ochils.

If not, retrace your steps to the crest of The Pirrack and slant diagonally to the right down the hillside. All of Tillicoultry is in full view all the way, so you'll have to work very hard to get lost!

LENGTH OF WALK: 2½ miles – allow 2 hours (but map-and-compass walkers will want to explore much further)

CONDITIONS: In good weather – easy persistent climb up Mill Glen. Many steps. Short, steep climb to top of The Pirrack. Steep descent on grass that can be slippery.

In bad weather or mist – views will be hidden, so it's not worth going higher than the head of Mill Glen.

GEAR: Take proper hiking boots, full hill-walking gear, hot drink, food – just in case

ACCOMMODATION AND REFRESHMENTS: Farriers, Alva House Stables, Woodland Park, Alva (3 miles from Tillicoultry) (0259 62702)

FURTHER READING: *Walks In The Ochils, Devon Valley Diary, Walking The Ochils And Beyond, Off The Beaten Track* – all by Richard Bernard, published by Clackmannan District Libraries, 17 Mar Street, Alloa FK10 1 HT, Central Region, Scotland (0259 722160)

On the Road to
'Many-towered Camelot'

THE LELAND TRAIL,
COLE TO CADBURY CASTLE, SOMERSET

Following the trail of the great itinerant,
John Somerville hops over a stile

Landscape doesn't come much greener than the rolling pastures of South Somerset, especially after a night's heavy rain. The cows of Cole Farm had spent the summer trampling the mud of the field gateways into hoof-pocked quagmires, over which silver sheets of rainwater now lay gleaming in the soft green of wet grass. To the north the pastureland rose as it met the outlying slopes of the Mendip Hills, and here the black skeleton trees of winter stood outlined against grey clouds thick with the threat of more rain.

The green, black and grey of this countryside had seemed unutterably depressing to me when, ten years old and unwillingly returning to my Dorset boarding school, I had contemplated it from the smoke-obscured windows of a railway carriage. But, thank Heaven, things change. Thirty intervening years had invested this landscape with sweeter associations. Instead of gulping miserable goodbyes to my father, I could meet him on this cold and spitting morning at the gate of Cole Station with the prospect of enjoying a good day's walk together.

The station had been converted into a smart private house since the old Somerset & Dorset line closed in 1966. We leaned over the gate to approve its renaissance before squaring away for Cole Farm and our rendezvous with the Leland Trail. Dad was looking well, lean and fit, a life-long scorner of wind and weather, ready as ever to walk the legs off me.

He set his customary clinking pace along the path as we climbed to the spine of Ridge Hill, pushing hard against a stiff breeze, our breath smoking behind us. Two buzzards wheeled in the wind, climbing in spirals on rock-steady wings above the deep valleys that curved below the ridge. The Leland Trail ran westwards, well provided with wooden stiles. The waymarks pointing out the route bore a likeness of John Leland in a tea-cosy hat, baggy eyes cast down and mouth set in a dyspeptic sulk. Not a pretty sight.

Poor Leland ended his life with his mental faculties all adrift, but he had been a bright and observant young man when he rode through England in the 1530s, listing the nation's antiquities on the orders of King Henry VIII. Leland's *Itinerary* recorded far more than antiquities: it set down for posterity the shape and character of Tudor England. The exact route that Leland rode through the West Country is a matter of conjecture, but South Somerset District Council's twenty-eight-mile Leland Trail from Alfred Tower to Ham Hill does its best to fill in some of the gaps.

On the eastern side of Castle Cary we dropped into Solomon's Lane, flanked by ancient holly trees, and splashed our way down to the town. The old Market House stood on doughty pillars, built sturdily of the local dark gold oolitic limestone known in these parts as hamstone. The George Hotel across the street sent out a seductive smell of cooking. Time for lunch.

'Hello, good morning, and a wet one,' smiled the lady behind the bar. A brace of plump solicitors filled the window seat, laying down the law to each other over their pints. A warm, somnolent place, the George, where no one minded our muddy boots on the floor or our rain-spattered anoraks thrown over the chairs. It was hard to face out again into the cold afternoon, but as we emerged the sun was pushing back the clouds from a brilliant blue patch of sky.

We turned into the lane curiously named Paddock Drain, and in a few strides between gold stone walls were out of the town and mounting the back of Lodge Hill. A vast sweep of a view widened behind us – the pimple of the distant tower on Glastonbury Tor and the finger of the nearer church tower over Evercreech village, backed by the cloud-covered bar of the Mendip Hills ten miles off. 'A very fair and fruteful champain,' had been Leland's comment, and by God he was right.

The green lanes and byways of this corner of Somerset all have their names, some recorded on the map: Corkscrew Lane, Frog Lane, Maggs Lane. On the far side of the Bruton road we plunged into Hicks's Lane, a sunken track running purposefully south and bending with the elastic roll of the land. Larks sang between damp earth and clear sky. A great and ancient subterranean city of badger tunnels pockmarked the sides of the lane, and beyond in a hollow the skeleton of an artesian well's windpump tower lay collapsed and rusting across the path.

In the road at the end of the green lane we got caught up in a stampede of sheep, a solid wedge of wool and mutton on the hoof, chased by a woman on a bike. 'Block that gap by the bridge for me, will you?' she called. Dad nipped smartly into the hedge to let them race by, and I hared off to reach the packhorse bridge just ahead of the tittuping flock.

The sheep clattered past, bleating madly and rolling their eyes sideways at me. Their agitated cries and the whistles and shouts of their pursuers floated to us, more and more faintly, as we picked our course through the squelching fields, past an old mill and down zigzag Sandbrook Lane into North Cadbury.

'I cam strayt to North-Cadbyri a village,' noted Leland, 'and about a mile farther to South-Cadbyri, and ther a litle beyond be great crestes of hylles.' His latterday trail-blazers have put an eastward bulge of two miles in their route here to take in the hamlet of Compton Pauncefoot, but with the rain beginning to freckle down once more Dad and I elected to follow more straightly in the hoofprints of the great Itinerant. We crossed the roaring A303 and passed South Cadbury's tiny Red Lion pub to find shelter in the little hamstone church at the end of its avenue of pollarded trees.

In the south aisle we stood, dripping and sniffing, admiring a medieval wall painting of a coped bishop with a belt round his waist and a mitre set atop his curly red hair. Some say it represents the martyred St Thomas à Becket, to whom the church was dedicated a hundred years or so after his death.

One of our cars was parked outside, ready to take us back to the other at Cole. But the grand finale of the walk was still to come. Behind the church rose the bald dome of Cadbury Castle, tonsured with trees, crowned with one of the truly memorable hill forts of Britain. We pounded up through the rings of ramparts to stand where men had stood on guard over the surrounding countryside from Neolithic to Norman times. What a view they commanded – north to Mendip, west over the Somerset Levels to Bridgwater Bay, south into Dorset and the Blackdown Hills, east across to the mighty ridge of Pen Hill.

'Camallate,' John Leland styled the fort, 'sumtyme a famose toun or castelle, apon a very torre or hille, wunderfully enstrengtheid of nature.' Was King Arthur's legendary court of Camelot once sited up here? Excavations in the 1960s uncovered the remains of a great feasting hall, and dated it to the sixth century. Local tales tell of ghostly horsemen riding from Cadbury Castle by night, their silver horseshoes glinting in the moonlight.

Who can say? For me, at dusk on this rainy winter afternoon, there was enough solid satisfaction in standing there silently beside my father, watching him gaze round the tremendous horizons of his native land.

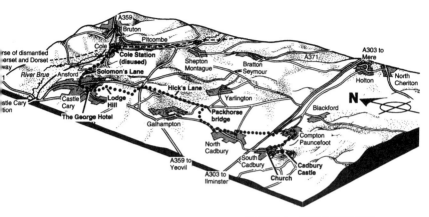

FACT FILE

MAP: OS 1:50,000 Landranger Sheet 183 'Yeovil and Frome'

Excellent larger-scale maps and walk notes in Leland Trail folder – available at £3.25 from the Chief Leisure and Arts Officer, South Somerset District Council, The Council Offices, Brympton Way, Yeovil, Somerset (0935 75272).

TRAVEL: From east – A303 to Wincanton, B3081 to Bruton, A359 towards Yeovil.

From south and west – A303 to Sparkford, A359 towards Bruton.

From north – A37 to Shepton Mallet, A371 and B3081 to Bruton.

Cole is 1 mile south-west of Bruton.

Nearest railway stations Bruton (2 m) and Castle Cary (3 m)

WALK DIRECTIONS: *Leland Trail – Stage 2* From Cole Station (670337) walk west down road to Cole Farm (665335); beyond farm, stile on right; Leland Trail waymarks show route over fields and across Ridge Hill to lane (651330). Turn left, then in 50 yards right into Solomon's Lane, leading to A371 (642328). Go right and cross road, left down Ansford road, right into Castle Cary's High Street to George Hotel (641323).

Leyland Trail – Stage 3 At corner of George turn left up Paddock Drain, over stile and up Lodge Hill. At summit pass to right of reservoir (642317), cross end of track to Manor Farm (642314) and follow waymarks to A359 (645310).

Turn left for 100 yards, then right along Hicks's Lane bridleway for over a mile to road (648293); walk ahead, then in 200 yards right over stile (648291) and through meadows to Sandbrook Lane (639287). Turn left and walk through North Cadbury. Cross A303 (631263) and reach St Thomas's Church in South Cadbury (632255).

Just past church go right up steep track to summit of Cadbury Castle (628251).

LENGTH OF WALK: 12 miles – allow 5 hours

CONDITIONS: Lanes, sunken tracks and field paths (some can be muddy)

GEAR: Walking boots; binoculars for the views from Lodge Hill and Cadbury Castle

REFRESHMENTS: George Hotel, Castle Cary; Catash Inn, North Cadbury; Red Lion, South Cadbury

ACCOMMODATION: George Hotel, Castle Cary (0963 50761)

FURTHER READING: John Leland's *Itinerary* (reprinted Centaur Press, 1964 – 5 vols)

In the Footsteps of a Good Shepherd

CARDINGMILL VALLEY, THE LONG MYND, SHROPSHIRE

'What? No crisps?' Cardingmill Valley sheep approach
in hopes of a titbit

Say what you like about mountain sheep, they do keep them-selves to themselves. You can't usually get within spitting distance of them, let alone offer them a titbit. The degraded specimens in the Cardingmill Valley, however, displayed no such admirable ovine reticence. They only left off nosing in the rubbish bins by the car park because they thought I might be concealing crisps about my person.

The moral fibre of the Cardingmill sheep has been rotted by too much exposure to too many summertime tourists. This deep, spectacular cleft in the eastern flank of the Long Mynd is, after all, one of Shropshire's prime beauty spots. But not another soul was in the valley on this cold, still winter's afternoon.

Down in the cosy teashops of Church Stretton the toasted teacakes were going well. Visitors were sprinkled in the pubs and antique shops, keeping to the warmth and light of the little spa town under the hills. I had the hard beauty of the Long Mynd entirely to myself.

I pushed the last sheep's muzzle out of my anorak pocket and climbed away up the stony path. The rounded, bracken-brown shoulders of the valley folded one behind another in front of me. They were sculpted into steep opposing slopes ten thousand years ago by Ice Age meltwaters rushing down from the roof of the Long Mynd. From the 1820s onwards the valley's stream powered a mill that carded Shropshire wool, but that industry is long gone from these hills.

Long Mynd stream valleys are 'batches' in local parlance. The batches snake and burrow into the sides of the 700-million-year-old hump of high ground, the rock bones of its skeleton sticking through its heathery skin, that rolls fifteen miles from north to south and four or five from east to west in parallel with the Caradoc Hills and Wenlock Edge. This undulating upland, with snug Church Stretton tucked into its eastern skirts, forms some of the loneliest hill country in England.

The footpath up the Cardingmill Valley is named Dr Mott's Road in honour of the Church Stretton physician who raised money to have it improved so that he could reach those of his patients who lived up on the bare back of the Long Mynd. Near the top of the batch the side valley of Lightspout Hollow swoops down with its fast-running stream to meet the good doctor's road.

Here I turned aside into Lightspout's wild cleft where red berries on the hawthorn bushes made the only splash of colour in a grey and rocky world. A rough track rose above old concrete spillways towards the growing sound of falling water.

The Lightspout waterfall was not at its fiercest after a month of little rain, but it was good to sit among the dried bracken fronds, soothed by its rustle, and look back down the plunging vee of the Hollow. Then it was up and on, scrambling up the rocky staircase beside the fall, plodding higher along a green path marked by many bootprints, mounting through sedge and bog to where the rolling brown face of the Long Mynd was turned to the grey sky.

A raven was flapping slowly overhead, uttering his harsh bark of a call, a bleak, austere sound that exactly fitted the scene – a dun-coloured ocean of heather and bracken, powdered with the faintest of snowfalls, rippling and waving off to a great disc of far horizon. I walked off the path for few hundred yards and stood looking round, thinking of the Reverend Donald Carr wading through head-high snowdrifts up here, bravely out-facing death.

In an idle moment in Church Stretton's Burway Bookshop I had bought the little paperback reprint of Mr Carr's heart-stopping account of his adventure on the Long Mynd on the night of 29 January 1865. With characteristically modest under-statement he called it *A Night in the Snow*. Some night. Some snow.

Donald Carr had two local parishes to look after: Woolstaston, just north of Church Stretton, and the remote moorland village of Ratlinghope four miles away on the far side of the hills. Mr Carr was a conscientious shepherd of his flock. He crawled on hands and knees through the snow drifts to get to Ratlinghope and take a service that afternoon. Then, struggling back across the Long Mynd, 'a furious gale came on, driving clouds of snow and icy sleet before it.' Iu was the vanguar of what turned out to be the worst blizzard for half a century.

In his introduction to *A Night in the Snow*, Mr Carr records his desire to set down every detail of his ordeal. Yet he knew, better than many a contemporary novelist, how to pace and structure his tale. Turning the pages in a Church Stretton tea-shop I had found myself chewing my nails in suspense. Now, looking over the scene of his tremendous battle for survival, the story sprang to life.

Mr Carr spent almost twenty-four hours wandering in huge snowdrifts through a pitch dark night and the following fog-bound day. The wind knocked him flat again and again. Several times he fell headlong down ravines hundreds of feet deep: '. . . a fearful glissade down a very precipitous place, and I was whirled round and round in my descent, sometimes head first, sometimes feet first, and again sideways, rolling over and over.'

He lost his hat and his gloves. His boots, still laced up, were torn off his feet by the suction of the drifts. Barefoot, snowblind and half dead from exposure, Mr Carr blundered at last into Lightspout Hollow. He survived a tumble over the upper part of the waterfall, and somehow crawled down to the bottom of the Cardingmill Valley.

The children who found him there ran away screaming, and no wonder. 'Doubtless,' mused the cleric, 'the head of a man protruding from a deep snow drift, crowned and bearded with ice like a ghastly emblem of winter, was a sight to cause panic.'

From the top of Lightspout Hollow I walked forward over the snow-dusted heather, picturing Mr Carr as he fought for life across those empty miles. Dr Mott's Road lay just ahead, and turning into its rutted course I was soon dropping down into the winding depths of the Cardingmill Valley. A scatter of lights twinkled below in the gathering dusk, beckoning me down to run the gauntlet of the mendicant sheep before regaining the bright streets of Church Stretton.

Walking into the town, looking forward to a cup of tea after my couple of cold hours on the Long Mynd, I thought again of the Revd Donald Carr. That hardy survivor had been given tea by the 'good kind people at the Carding Mill' at the end of his tribulations, before making his way back home.

Mr Carr saved his badly frostbitten fingers by 'the use of cold water and continued friction'. He had an uncomfortable few weeks while hundreds of gorse prickles worked their way out of his hands and feet. Then he wrote his little book, donated the profits to Woolstaston Church restoration fund, thanked God for keeping him awake through that awful night, and put the whole matter behind him.

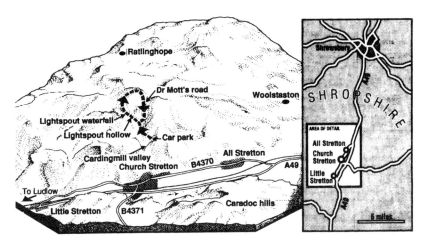

FACT FILE

MAP: OS 1:50,000 Landranger Sheet 137 'Ludlow and Wenlock Edge'

TRAVEL: A49 south from Shrewsbury or north from Ludlow to Church Stretton. Turn off into town to top of street; turn right on B4370. Lane to Cardingmill Valley is signposted on left in a few hundred yards. Park here, or higher up valley at car park.

Nearest railway station: Church Stretton.

WALK DIRECTIONS: From car park (441949) walk up valley for ½ mile to bear left up Lightspout Hollow where its stream joins that of Cardingmill Valley (435951). Walk up to waterfall (429951). Scramble up steep rocks on right of fall; path reappears at top. Where stream divides take right-hand fork, following green path on right bank to top of valley. Make for a post sticking up ahead, and continue forward for ¼ mile to meet Dr Mott's Road (427958). Turn right to descend into Cardingmill Valley.

LENGTH OF WALK: 3 miles – allow 2 hours.

CONDITIONS: Rough tracks; some stiff short climbs; steep scramble by Lightspout waterfall. Don't try this walk in a blizzard!

GEAR: Good boots and waterproofs. Take a compass in case of mist on the top.

REFRESHMENTS: Plenty of places in Church Stretton

ACCOMMODATION: The Old Rectory, Hopesay, near Craven Arms (058 87 245)

FURTHER READING: *A Night in the Snow* by Revd E. Donald Carr (Clark & Howard Books, 4 Merridale Gardens, Wolverhampton WV3 0UX) – available from Burway Bookshop, Church Stretton

The Unstoppable March of the Marshes

WELLS-NEXT-THE-SEA TO BLAKENEY, NORTH NORFOLK

The waterfront at Blakeney

Egret was not looking her best. Crusted with rust and salt, she creaked wearily at her mooring ropes. The big bags of fertilizer had been swung out of her hold and lay heaped on the quayside. One of her crew sat hunched against the early morning chill in a bo'sun's chair slung from her bows, scowling as he dabbed paint over the blemishes left by the night passage from Holland across a roughish and mist-shrouded North Sea. Freighters wanting to make their way up the silty mile-long channel to Wells-next-the-Sea, North Norfolk's one remaining working port, have to catch the right spring tide.

Wells's handful of inshore boats was still at sea, and the waterfront slumbered. The old brick granaries and warehouses stood silent. An old man with hands pushed deep into jacket pockets lounged wordlessly, watching *Egret*'s shivering painter. A fisherman with a rod across his handlebars biked slowly away towards his day's sport. The clank of his bicycle chain came clearly across the brimming water in Wells Harbour as I set out eastwards along a sea wall nearly two miles inland of an invisible sea.

The little ports of this North Norfolk coast – Wells, Brancaster, Blakeney, Cley – were prosperous wool towns in medieval times. But over the centuries they have been fighting a losing battle with the slowly growing marshes that have choked off their harbours one by one. The Landranger map tells the story. The villages lie well inland along a string of road that skirted the sea in former days. Now their silent quays look out on great aprons of salt marshes, a twenty-five-mile strip of them in an almost unbroken line from Hunstanton on the Wash right round to Sheringham.

Longshore drift is the villain of the piece, a gradual building-up of offshore shingle banks by the prevailing west-flowing tide. The silt that washes seaward down the Glaven and Stiffkey rivers piles up behind the shingle banks, a fertile bed for the growth of long-rooted plants like spartina grass and sea purslane that consolidate the ever-spreading marshes.

From the sea wall beyond Wells I stared out across a solid mile of drab brown marshland to a dark line of Corsican pines on the edge of sight, apparently growing well out to sea. They were planted to prevent the waves recapturing a slice of rich farmland reclaimed in Victorian times. But no one nowadays would dream of turning these bare marshes into grazing fields. The coast ports' misfortune is a godsend to nature-lovers, particularly bird watchers. The North Norfolk marshes are one gigantic nature reserve, where hundreds of species of geese, ducks and waders, hawks and songbirds come and go according to their kind at various times of the year.

There were notices below the sea wall, warning would-be voyeurs of bird life about the dangers of being trapped on the marshes by flood tides. I stayed on the raised wall, trying to steady my binoculars in the wind. Groups of birds flashed across the lenses – a tight bunch of wigeon speeding out to their day-time sea roosts with a flicker of white wing patches, chestnut-breasted shelduck flapping ponderously down to the invertebrate-crammed muds of the tideline, thousands of tiny knot swirling in midge-like clouds. My eyeballs ached from swivelling in pursuit of streaking targets.

I turned inland up a rutted lane and found myself on the coast road opposite St John's Church on the outskirts of Stiffkey village. 'Stew-kie,' enunciate visitors not quite sufficiently in the know. 'Stew-kie' it is, local people say – but only when praising the famous Stiffkey Blue cockles.

Flint cobbles and old red brick combine handsomely at Stiffkey, a tiny place that has seen more than its share of unconventional and widely misunderstood residents. Henry Williamson, author of *Tarka the Otter*, left his beloved North Devon to settle here in 1937. He took on the run-down Old Hall Farm in the valley below the church and wrestled it into good shape, driving himself and his family to the edge of despair and beyond in the process. 'Nearly every day in Norfolk was a little death,' Williamson wrote later.

Then there was poor Revd Harold Davidson, a victim of bigotry in the 1930s. Nowadays, rather than being thrown out of his living at Stiffkey, Mr Davidson would be applauded for his efforts to save the souls of London prostitutes. He became a menagerie showman, publicizing his innocence as 'Daniel in the Lions' Den', and met a sad, bizarre end in July 1937, mauled to death by one of his lions in front of a crowd on Skegness sea front.

'We remember him well,' said the lady who was dusting the pews in St John's. 'People are only interested in the scandal, but he was a kind man, and much loved here.'

Back on Stiffkey Marshes there was ungentlemanly behaviour going on. A little band of dark-bellied brent geese was being given a hard time by four bird watchers old enough to know better. They whooped and screamed, waving their arms and rushing across the marsh to make the brents get up and fly. After watching this exhibition cautiously for some time, the geese took to the air and went off to saner surroundings. As they disappeared I had the smug satisfaction of seeing one of the screamers trip up and take a nosedive into a particularly muddy creek.

A watery sun was beginning to get the better of the low cloud as I trudged past the yachts lying in the mud at Morston Quay, heading for the huddled red roofs of Blakeney. There were good bold sailors in Tudor Blakeney, men who thought nothing of venturing to Iceland for the fishing. These days the twisting streets of the old flint village run down to a quayside entirely given over to pleasure craft. Like Morston to the west and Cley to the east, the creeping marshes have done for Blakeney's sea trade.

Blakeney's two-towered church is dedicated to St Nicholas, the patron saint of fishermen. In the church's slender subsidiary tower (no one is quite sure what it was built for) a light is still kept burning by night as it always has been, for the guidance of seafarers. St Nicholas's must rank as the friendliest church in Norfolk with its displays of village history, its home-made produce for sale, its cheerful notices and welcoming church-wardens. From one of them I collected the key to the main tower and spiralled up to the top.

As if by appointment the sun let down a pale beam as I came out of the stair door. A rich brown tint flushed the grey of the marshes below, pressed like a broad hand across the mouths of the coastal villages to block off the salty breath of commerce. Across Blakeney Harbour's dried-out pan the long shingle arm of Blakeney Point, a renowned landfall for rare migrating birds, stretched back towards Wells-next-the-Sea, the sky above it alive with geese and lapwings.

It has taken Blakeney Point the best part of a thousand years to reach its present length of something over four miles. In another thousand the western tip of its finger will be stopping the harbour mouth at Wells. As I leaned out a hundred feet above the ground, gazing round at immensities of marsh and sky, there didn't seem to be much point in worrying about that just yet.

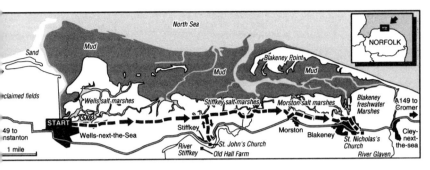

FACT FILE

MAP: OS 1:50,000 Landranger Sheets 132 'North West Norfolk' and 133 'North East Norfolk'.

TRAVEL: A149 from Hunstanton or Cromer to Wells-next-the-Sea. Park on waterfront.

NB No trains, infrequent buses from Blakeney to Wells. Taxi: (0328) 710294 (Mr Rix).

WALK DIRECTIONS: From Wells waterfront walk east down East Quay (918438) and continue straight ahead along sea wall. After 3½ miles take lane inland (973440) to Stiffkey Church (974430). Return to coast path and continue east through Morston Quay (006443) to Blakeney waterfront (027441) and church (033436).

Blakeney church tower: open every Friday, 2.30 to dusk – tea and welcome laid on. Open at other times by arrangement – contact Mrs Anne Doughty, 2 The Butts, Saxlingham Road, Blakeney NR25 7PB.

LENGTH OF WALK: 9 miles – allow 4 hours

CONDITIONS: Sea wall path (can be muddy) and lanes

GEAR: Warm clothing, binoculars, bird book, camera

REFRESHMENTS: Golden Fleece, Wells; Red Lion, Stiffkey; Blakeney Hotel

107

ACCOMMODATION: Blakeney – Manor Hotel (0263 740376); Blakeney Hotel (0263 740797); Morston – Morston Hall Country House Hotel (0263 741041)

FURTHER READING: *The Story of a Norfolk Farm* by Henry Williamson (Faber, 1941)
National Trust booklet guide to Blakeney Point (available locally)
Blakeney village and church guides (available in Blakeney Church)

Heaven at the End of the Central Line

PERIVALE WOOD AND HORSENDEN HILL
MIDDLESEX

A tangle of trees and hedgerow in ancient Perivale Wood

As the Central Line's tarnished silver tube train clacked west from Hanger Lane, the itinerant busker with the guitar swung into 'Knocking On Heaven's Door'. The only passenger beside myself to have come this far snorted and raised his eyes to the carriage roof, if not quite to Heaven's Door.

I gazed past his crossly rattled *Sun* and out of the smeary windows of the train to see Horsenden Hill's wooded dome rising over the factories and close-packed roofs of Perivale. On that circular hump of hilly ground, hemmed in on all sides by suburban west London, an ancient rural landscape lay miraculously preserved, ripe for exploration on this bracing blue winter morning.

At Perivale station I disembarked and followed my disgruntled fellow-traveller up Horsenden Lane. The green slope of the hill stood ahead, flooded with sunshine. The strollers of Perivale were dotted across its grassy acres with half London spread at their feet, and I was tempted to climb straight up there and join them. But close at hand, hidden behind the semi-detached houses, lay another fragment of an older and wilder landscape, Horsenden Hill's own heavenly gateway.

At the turn of the century Perivale was a tiny settlement of thirty inhabitants. 'A rustic, deeply-secluded hamlet,' noted the local historian J. Allen Brown in 1890, 'with a few red-tiled farmhouses, toned down into unison with the hedgerows and trees, the survival of a medieval village but eleven miles from St Paul's.' Most of the parish's farms grew hay for horse fodder, supplying both capital and Army. Life inched along at a rural pace.

But then the factories came west – Sanderson's the wallpaper manufacturers in 1929, Hoover's a couple of years later. Houses sprang up like mushrooms, covering the hayfields and obliterating the farms. Wembley and Ealing, Greenford and Sudbury reached out and swallowed the little hamlet. They would have swallowed the last remnant of the great Wood of Perivale, where medieval grandees once hunted stag and wild boar, if the Selborne Society of naturalists had not already taken it over as a nature reserve. I had come to Perivale a fully paid-up member of the Selborne Society (to join, see p. 114), with the right to explore Perivale Wood to my heart's content.

At Perivale Library I collected the key to the reserve gate, and was lord of twenty-seven acres of oak, crab apple, ash and rowan, of field, wood, marsh and pond, of goldcrests and redwings, of a maze of winding paths softened by dry leaves in which my footfalls were as muffled as the distant hum of London beyond the trees.

Bundles of hazel poles, coppiced earlier, had been stacked against the oak trunks of Perivale Wood. A woodpecker cackled overhead among the branches. I followed a path beside a hedge, the ancient boundary marker between the parishes of Perivale and Greenford, that was already old when Plantagenets were on the throne of England. The Selborne Society's booklet listed the trees it contained – elm, field maple, hazel, blackthorn, hawthorn, spindle, elder. I could never have told them apart in this leafless season, but it was enough to know they were there.

It was too early in the year for the wood's famous carpet of bluebells to be on show, but for compensation I had the squirrels bouncing among bare branches and the moorhens skulking on rushy ponds. At the top of the wood a gate let me out on to the towpath of the Grand Union Canal, where I startled a cruising coot into an undignified squawking dive.

The canal reached Perivale in 1801 as the navvies drove it south from Oxford to the Thames. Barges took the hay from the Perivale farms up to London, and brought down cargoes of the city's rubbish which were tipped in a corner of Perivale Wood. These days the old rubbish heap is a green mound smothered with elder bushes where I picked up a delicate bone-china cup, its sides fluted and its handle elegantly crooked.

Beyond the hump-backed canal bridge the broad footpaths of Horsenden Hill led up among thorn thickets. Their hazel hedges had been neatly cut and laid in traditional fashion, the horizontal pleachers or whip-thin stems woven between upright stakes. On the sloping field called Home Mead the pale green grasses, silvered by the low sun, were thick with dry sprays of dead knapweed and crisp brown docks, sapless and weightless, swaying in the wind.

I strolled a slow circuit of Horsenden's flat top. At 276 feet the hill is little more than a bump, but London lies low. Six counties and ten London boroughs were there for the spotting. The enormous view spun by – the Surrey hills in the south a long blue line under the glare of the sun, Middlesex fading off into the west to where the houses gave way to a thin strip of Berkshire, Harrow on its hill to the north. In the east London stretched away, ten miles of roofs and windows, towers and chimneys, to one speck among a thousand on the skyline that might have been the dome of St Paul's Cathedral.

Seventy years ago the southerly view from Horsenden Hill was of hedged fields, farms and woods, a rural patchwork. Thanks to the far-sightedness of the Middlesex county councillors of the 1930s, who bought Horsenden to safeguard it from the oncoming tide of buildings, that long-established landscape still clings to the shoulders and skirts of the hill.

These days Ealing Borough Council has the care of those 250 acres of green oasis. A golf course has encroached from the eastern side, but the ancient oaks and hornbeams of Horsenden Wood stand undisturbed. The coppices are still harvested and properly managed, the hay crop still gathered from Horsenden's fields.

Things are not just left to grow jungly on the hill. Scrub is cut by hand, wildflower seeds scattered, introduced trees such as sycamores felled to let the native hazels and willows return. 'Wonderful work,' said the woman on the path down from summit. 'But it's not officially green belt. What if the council ever decided to sell it off? I'd like to think it was really *safe* – but these days, you know . . .'

I picked a path from the Horsenden Hill guide book and found myself deep in what had once been the formally laid out gardens of Rohais House. The house was pulled down in the 1940s, leaving the tangled Japanese bamboos, the laurels and privets to grow wild. There was a semicircle of brickwork by the path as a reminder of a vanished well, a flight of steps leading nowhere, a retaining wall with ivy drooping where the herbaceous borders flowered.

The path snaked out of the garden jungle to cross the big hayfields at the foot of the hill – Wood Field, Rockware Field, The Pightle. Bursting with wildlife in summer, the meadows now lay flat, green and silent in the long rays of a chilly sunset. I crossed them at a contented snail's pace, hands in pockets and eyes turned to the crown of Horsenden Hill, thinking of the legend of beautiful Ealine.

Daughter of the Saxon chief Horsa (did he bequeath his name to Horsenden Hill?), Ealine married the boorish, drunken and lecherous Bren. When Horsa received a plea for help from his daughter – brought to him by a talking starling – he sallied forth against his son-in-law. Both men were slain in the ensuing battle, and Horsenden Hill was heaped up above the grave of Horsa. On misty, moonlit nights the old warrior stalks abroad,

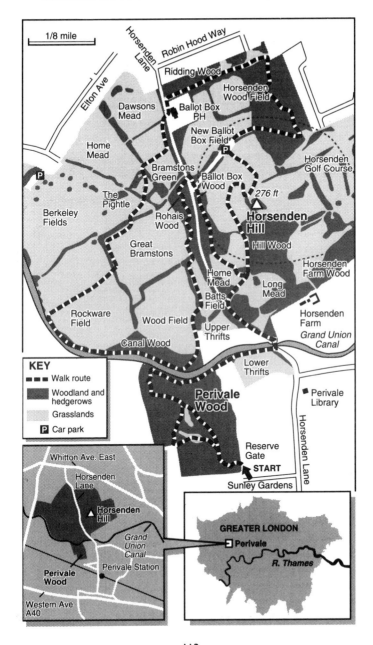

1/8 mile

Horsenden Lane
Robin Hood Way
Ridding Wood
Elton Ave
Dawsons Mead
Ballot Box PH
Horsenden Wood Field
New Ballot Box Field
Home Mead
Bramstons Green
Ballot Box Wood
Horsenden Golf Course
The Pightle
Rohais Wood
276 ft
Horsenden Hill
Berkeley Fields
Great Bramstons
Hill Wood
Horsenden Farm Wood
Home Mead
Long Mead
Batts Field
Rockware Field
Wood Field
Upper Thrifts
Horsenden Farm
Grand Union Canal
Canal Wood
Lower Thrifts
Perivale Library
Horsenden Lane

KEY
- ▪▪▪ Walk route
- Woodland and hedgerows
- Grasslands
- P Car park

Perivale Wood

Reserve Gate
START
Sunley Gardens

Whitton Ave. East
Horsenden Lane
Horsenden Hill
Grand Union Canal
Perivale Station
Perivale Wood
Western Ave A40

GREATER LONDON
Perivale
R. Thames

113

while his steed can be heard tramping a roundabout course under the hill.

My own roundabout trampings were almost at an end. I crossed Bramston's Green, took a last look up at the darkening bulk of Horsenden Hill, and entered the splendiferous portico of the Ballot Box pub – a heavenly door of yet another kind.

FACT FILE

MAP: Use those in guides to Perivale Wood and Horsenden Hill (see below).

TRAVEL: Central Line tube to Perivale

WALK DIRECTIONS: Pick your own route from many suggested in the guides

LENGTH OF WALK: Perivale Wood and Horsenden Hill 3–5 miles – allow 2–3 hours

CONDITIONS: Some paths muddy, especially among trees. *NB* Key to Perivale Wood nature reserve available from Perivale Library, only to visitors already members of the Selborne Society. To join Society, contact the Secretary (081 578 3181)

GEAR: Stout footwear; binoculars for view from hill

REFRESHMENTS: The Ballot Box, at northern foot of hill

FURTHER READING: Perivale Wood reserve guide – contact Selborne Society (081 578 3181)
Horsenden Hill Countryside Walk guide – from Ealing Borough Council (081 579 2424)
A Farm in Perivale by Eva Farley, and *The Chronicles of Greenford Parva* by J. Allen Brown – both in Perivale Library (081 997 2830): open Tue and Fri 9.00–7.45. Thurs and Sat 9.00–5.00

Copse and Robbers

EAST KIELDER BURN AND KIELDERHEAD, NORTHUMBERLAND

Kielder Head Farm lies abandoned under the slopes of the
Northumbrian moors

When a Charlton chief sat down to dinner in times gone by
and found a spur on the table where his meal should have
been, he knew the cupboard was bare once more. His wife was
telling him to saddle up and steal a fresh batch of cattle from his
neighbours' herds. The families of North Tynedale in west-
ernmost Northumberland – Charltons and Robsons, Milburns
and Dodds – were never slow to lay hands on each other's
property in the lawless old days. Here where the Scottish border
ran across the Cheviot Hills, far from civilization, 'reiving' or
cattle-thieving was a way of life.

Remoteness is still the keynote of this region, but a Charlton
reiving party would be hard put to it these days to work up a
good gallop along the upper reaches of the North Tyne River.
Since 1926 the western fringes of the Cheviots have been planted

with 250 square miles of close-packed conifers, while in their depths sprawl the seven miles of the Kielder Water reservoir, Europe's largest man-made lake.

I found it hard to picture what kind of landscape those statistics might have shaped, until I opened the Ordnance Survey map to find half of it coloured green with a great blue stain in the centre. Kielder Water is beautiful, and the Kielder trees formidably impressive in their domination of the hills. But by the time I had turned off the road from Bellingham at Kielder village and driven up the bumpy Forest Drive to East Kielder Farm, I was longing for the sight of something other than water and trees.

Relief was at hand. The farm stands on a spur of moorland on the northern edge of the forest, and within ten minutes I had turned my back on the corduroy battalions of trees and was striding under a still, cloudy sky over tussocks of rush and coarse grass with my face to the long, bare shoulders of open hillside that flank the winding shallows of the East Kielder Burn.

The footpath that runs with the burn is not one of those carefully waymarked and leafleted by the Forestry Commission. There are few attractions for the Kielder tourist here. The burn threads a wild and inhospitable crevice of the hills, where the wind blows cold and the sense of isolation grows with each lonely mile. Walking here, you leave the twentieth century behind on the outskirts of the forest and enter the unreconstructed emptiness in which the reivers and cross-border raiders of the past could operate unhindered.

I squelched across tiny burns running in black channels of peat, and stood looking down from the hillside on to the grey roofs of Scaup Farm. The hollow barking of a dog came from one of the stone sheds, but there was no sign of life around the buildings. Scaup is certainly one of the loneliest farms in England, tucked down in the shelter of the hills with Kielder Forest's dark mass blocking its southward view and the narrowing valley of the burn filling half the sky to the north.

The East Kielder Burn divides here into Scaup Burn and White Kielder Burn. I dropped down the hill to ford White Kielder upstream of the ruined farmstead of Kielder Head, where a line of stunted alders, shaggy with lichen, leaned over their leafless reflections in the peat-brown water. Spring comes late to this windbitten and rain-soaked valley. But there were new-born lambs in the sheep pens of Scaup, and a cheery 'Hello now!' from the farmer and his wife tending them.

Those were the last human voices I heard all day. No one lives up here in the cleft of the White Kielder Burn. The rough land is altogether too harsh and unyielding, giving sustenance only to sheep, and to the conifers high on the flanks of East Kielder Moor and Grey Mare Knowe, immense sweeps of hillside to right and left of the valley.

The footpath on the left bank of the burn was little better than a sheep track, but there were clues to its former importance as a droving road over the hills to Byrness in Redesdale. Large boulders stood out beside the path as grey blobs in the featureless sheets of pale grass, and flat stones had been placed as bridges across the burns, their backs hollowed by the tread of feet through the centuries.

Following these now disregarded signs of past activity along the old path, I traversed the hillside and came down to a crumbling stone sheepfold with the roofless remains of a shepherd's hut built into one wall. The tiny single room was jammed with the mossy timbers of disused sheep pens, but the little iron fire grate that once warmed the hardy men who worked here was still set in the foot of the hut's tottering gable end, and the massive stone lintel had not yet fallen from its place above the doorway.

A dipper flew up from the burn as I emerged from the hut, his white breast flashing as he darted downstream. Somewhere ahead in the crags of Kielderhead Moor a hawk was whistling, a piercing sound in the lonely valley, overlain for a few heart-stopping moments by the snarl of a jet that streaked into and out of sight in ten seconds. That jarring manifestation of furious technology seemed as remote and ridiculous as a dream, as silence settled down again on Kielderhead and the hawk's whistle came down from the moors.

The valley of the White Kielder Burn steepened again as I trudged north, its curves tightening all the way. Now the path ran through heather high above the burn, past circular sheep-folds long disused and over the stony beds of side streams where the grass hung smooth and inviting, concealing ankle-breaking drops. More than once I went skidding through these treacherous mats and came down hard on my backside with my legs in a burn. Kielderhead is not the place for a careless walker.

A mile above the shepherd's hut the hillsides ceased their upward rolling and curved together to form a dead-end valley of broad-breasted slopes five miles from the nearest tarmac road, hidden deep in the folds of the moors. The old drover's road turned aside here and climbed under the rock faces of White Crags to continue its lonely course over Girdle Fell and down into Redesdale.

I could have gone with it, giving myself four blissful miles of upland walking followed by as many miserable hours of fruitless searching for return transport to East Kielder Farm. Instead, I lay back in the heather and savoured the trickles of the burn and the crisp smell of peat-laden ground. Not a sign of spring had yet penetrated this secret valley, but another month would put that right. There were five miles of return tramping to face, but they, too, could wait awhile.

FACT FILE

MAP: OS 1:50,000 Landranger Sheet 80 'The Cheviot Hills'

TRAVEL: From west – M6 to Carlisle, A7 to Canonbie, B6357 to Newcastleton and Saughtree (561967), minor road to Kielder. From east – A68 to West Woodburn (893868 – 16 miles N of Corbridge), minor road to Bellingham and Kielder. At Kielder follow signs to Kielder Castle and take Forest Drive. In 2 miles (651959) stony Scaup Farm track continues ahead; Forest Drive bends right to reach East Kielder Farm (658959).

WALK DIRECTIONS: From East Kielder Farm, faint paved track runs diagonally uphill away from Forest Drive to reach two gates in angle of stone wall by small shed. Continue north above East Kielder Burn for 2 miles to

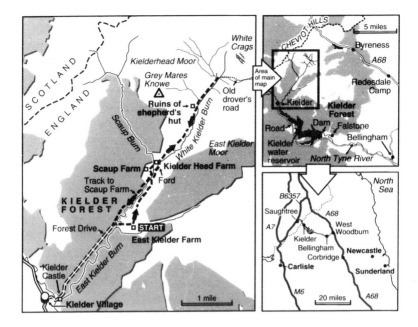

descend opposite Scaup Farm (664978). Ford right-hand water (White Kielder Burn) just above ruined Kielder Head Farm (666980) by alder trees – line of convenient stones in burn.

NB If burn is in spate or is very powerful and noisy after heavy rain, don't try to ford it – your walk ends here!

Continue up path on west bank of White Kielder Burn for 3 miles to meeting of burns under Kielderhead Moor (687009).

Return route can be varied from Scaup Farm by going through farmyard and keeping to west bank of East Kielder Burn along farm road,

LENGTH OF WALK: 10 miles – allow 4–5 hours

CONDITIONS: After very heavy rain or in mist, curtail walk at Scaup. Tell someone where you are going and when you expect to be back. Paths are narrow in heather and rough grass, and can be slippery. Two burns to ford. Two barbed-wire sheep fences – first one must be scrambled over.

GEAR: Full hill-walking gear; binoculars

REFRESHMENTS: Kielder Working Men's Club

ACCOMMODATION: Blackcock Inn, Falstone (8 miles from Kielder towards Bellingham) (0434 240200)

FURTHER INFORMATION: Kielder Castle Visitor Centre (0434 250209)

The Flowery Hills of Clare

THE BURREN WAY
CO. CLARE, IRELAND

Jogging along through the Burren's timeless landscape

In the evening the naked limestone of the hilltops around Ballyvaughan had glistened grey and empty under the Atlantic rain driving in from Galway Bay. But by morning sweet sunshine had crept over County Clare, the bloody cranesbill had opened as if at a heavenly command and the Burren lay basking, its rocky face spattered with fresh purple from crest to crest.

Setting out from Ballyvaughan along the Burren Way I was intent on shaking the stiffness out of my legs. The previous day I had wandered the best part of twenty miles into the stony wastes of the Burren in pelting rain showers, in search of prehistoric wedge tombs and the ruins of ring forts and medieval churches.

They had not been hard to find. Though nowadays these 375 square miles of glacier-scraped and weather-smoothed limestone uplands and valleys are entirely silent and depopulated, there was a time – before they had been scourged by Cromwellian fire and sword – when monks, teachers, musicians and lore-masters made the Burren one of Ireland's centres of culture and learning. The ruins of their buildings lie everywhere – by the roadsides, on the terraced flanks of the hills, smothered in undergrowth in forgotten side valleys.

I had had my fill, and a little over, of grey stone relics, but three miles out of Ballyvaughan on this bright spring morning the sunlight slanted seductively across the chunky tower of the 400-year-old Newtown Castle under Cappanawalla Hill. I turned off the lane to enter the blackened belly of the tower, climbing a shaky spiral stairway past cylindrical rooms with domed ceilings to reach the topmost chamber, its grassy floor a mass of buttercups and forget-me-nots, its stone windows with their crumbling mullions framing the dusty track of the Burren Way as it ran out of sight beyond the slope of Cappanawalla.

I walked fast along the level lane, tramping away the last twinges of yesterday's rain-soaked miles. The ivy-draped gables and wildly overgrown graveyard of Rathborney Church went by; then at a fork in the road the Burren Way struck out for the heights.

A stiff climb up a snaking, stone-walled boreen (as the laneways of Ireland are called) landed me without warning on a saddle of high ground above an immense cleft cut by the Caher River, a thousand feet down through the soft tissue of the limestone. The Burren Way between its boreen walls slipped out of sight over the rim of the hillside, to reappear as a green and grey thread twining up the far slope.

Down on the stone-littered banks of the Caher River the valley lay in shadow, but there was no coolness there. The limestone trapped the heat and dried my throat to sandpaper. A very old man hobbled slowly to his gate with a mug of water dipped from a bucket in his scullery. ''Tis the sweetest well in Ireland that this water comes from,' he murmured, 'up there above on the hill. I fetch it every day. Have you enough, now?'

The cool well-water put new energy into me for the climb up into the sunlight and the flayed white highlands of limestone. From the next saddle at a thousand feet I looked forward on to another stunning prospect; west across Galway Bay to the three low, stony blades of the Aran Islands, cutting the open water in blue heat haze fifteen miles off, and even further into the south where the Cliffs of Moher ran their long square snouts out into the sea above collars of foam.

There was a sea breeze to take the sting out of the sun as I gazed round over a score of miles of white limestone, terraced and domed into the characteristic rounded hills of the Burren. I climbed the boreen wall, got the flower book out of my pack and gave myself up to an hour's concentrated gryke-grubbing.

Grykes are the deep fissures between the rectangular sections or clints into which the limestone sheets cracked during prehistoric earth movements. There is no habitat in the world quite like the clints and grykes of the Burren when it comes to mind-boggling varieties of flowering plants.

Why plants normally found in arctic and alpine places happily flourish in the Burren alongside Mediterranean species, or how lime-loving plants can grow in the same ground as those that need acid soils, is one of those mysteries no one has been able to explain. The mild climate, the warmth of the Gulf Stream that enwraps the Burren and the sunlight rebounding from clint into gryke probably all play their part.

Today I couldn't be bothered with the why and the wherefore; the flowers were there, and they were beautiful. I had come to the Burren too late in the year to find the spectacular blue spring gentians, but there were thick drifts of pink, white and purple orchids, and each pale yellow flower of mountain avens cupped its drop of yesterday's rainwater. The water bubbled and chuckled deep in the grykes, from whose shade the pale green leaves of maidenhair fern and the long spurs of harts'-tongue poked up, greedy for sunlight.

I teetered across the Burren moonscape, loose clints wobbling under my boots, flower book in hand and nose to the limestone, blind to everything but the ferns and flowers. Breda and her father must have been watching me from their picnic spot under the boreen wall for quite some time before they broke in on my absorption, calling to know if I'd like a cup of tea.

Dark-haired, freckle-faced Breda can't have been more than

six years old, but her manners were impeccable. She opened a tin, cajoling me: 'My mother made the soda bread. Go on, take two – we've plenty.' Her father smiled proudly, ruffling Breda's hair. He had been in England himself, working in Nottingham. The English were fine people, but they wouldn't talk to you. It was just their way, so. Well – goodbye, and God bless!

As soon as I had turned the corner I heard English voices coming up the boreen. A couple marched by, striding with chins out and eyes averted. No words of greeting passed. I was glad Breda and her father couldn't see this very English ritual.

Now the Burren Way began its long descent off the hilltops, running purposefully south-west and shedding height gently. The stony boreen became a tarred lane, undulating over the final rise and falling past tiny farmsteads. Ballinalacken Castle reared its jagged head out of a thicket of trees like a fairy tale. I held steadily on, down from the scoured world of limestone into the lush green lands of the Clare coastline where Doolin village straggled along its dead-end road to the sea.

What the Burren heights are to the botanist, Doolin is to lovers of Irish traditional music. There were fiddlers swapping tunes on the bridge over the Aille River as I walked into the village, accordion players twiddling away on the benches outside McGann's pub. A glass of creamy-headed black stout stood at every elbow. Inside the bar I could hear other musicians tuning up.

The old man's well-water and Breda's buttered soda bread had done their best for me, but something more fortifying was beckoning. I strolled towards McGann's, feeling all of a sudden tired and thirsty, as the first reel of the evening came floating out of the doorway.

FACT FILE

MAP: Irish OS ½ inch: 1 mile Sheet 14 'Galway Bay'

'The Burren' (1.8 inch: 1 mile) in Tim Robinson's 'Folding Landscape' series is of much more practical use.

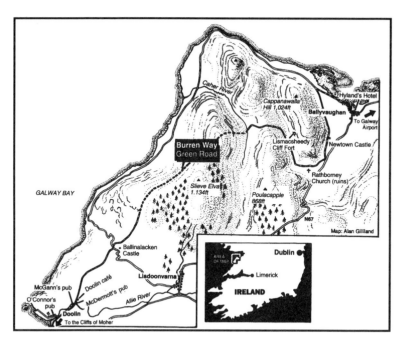

Leaflet guide 'The Burren Way' is based on Robinson's map.

All these maps and guides available from Tourism Group, Shannon Development (010 353 61 361555) or Tourist Information Offices locally.

TRAVEL: Aer Lingus (081 569 5555) from London and major UK regional airports to Galway Airport; then N18 south to Kilcolgan, N67 west to Ballyvaughan (28 miles from Galway Airport).

WALK DIRECTIONS: Leaving Hyland's Hotel in Ballyvaughan (230077), walk right to quay and follow coast road to turn left (210088) on track to Newtown Castle (215064). Continue to crossroads (214050); turn right to pass Rathborney Church ruins on your left (205046) and then Lismacsheedy hillfort ruins high on right (192070). Just beyond, fork left (191070 – 'Cathair an Aird Reis' sign) up boreen, over saddle of hill and down to cross road (173070).

Bear right and immediately left to cross Caher River, then immediately right again (Green Road and Burren Way signs) to climb over another saddle and descend to road (134043). Turn left, then right to join another road

125

(130039); in ¼ of a mile keep ahead at left-hand bend and continue to pass Ballinalacken Castle on your left (102004). At L54 road (100002) turn left and immediately right along road to reach bridge at Doolin (080974).

LENGTH OF WALK: 15 miles – allow 6 hours

CONDITIONS: Easy up-and-down walking (yellow arrow waymarks) on roads and stony tracks

GEAR: Strong boots; food and drink; good flower book

REFRESHMENTS: None en route. Ballyvaughan – Hyland's Hotel. Doolin – McGann's, McDermott's or O'Connor's; Doolin Café.

ACCOMMODATION: Hyland's Hotel, Ballyvaughan (010 353 65 77037); Maeve Fitzerald, Churchfield, Doolin (010 353 65 74209)

FURTHER READING: *Burren Journey* by George Cunningham
The Burren by Mary Angela Keane (Irish Heritage Series No. 30)

FURTHER INFORMATION: Irish Tourist Board, 150–151 New Bond Street, London W1Y 0AQ (071 493 3201)

A Million Miles Away from Purgatory

BRADFORD-ON-AVON, WILTSHIRE

A narrowboat chugging along the Kennet and Avon
near Bradford-on-Avon

In the dank darkness of the little old lock-up on Bradford-on-Avon's Town Bridge, seven-year-old Elizabeth had the welfare of erstwhile malefactors on her mind. 'But where did they go to the *loo*?' was her pertinent question. Our guide was ready with the answer. 'Down that hole there,' he said briskly, indicating a grim stone chute opening on the River Avon below. Elizabeth peered down the hole. 'Ugh!' she said, grinning with horrified delight.

Taking two young children for a Sunday afternoon walk can be a fair foretaste of purgatory, as every parent knows. The best-laid plans in what promises to be the ideal location are apt to founder in the face of tiredness, thirst and full bladders. But

Bradford-on-Avon caters for all that, and a good deal more. The little Wiltshire town and its waterside walk to Avoncliff are made for the job.

Mellow stone houses stand piled on the hill overlooking the Avon as it slides beneath Town Bridge. Bradford was a well-to-do wool and cloth manufacturing town from medieval times until early this century, and there's still an air of prosperous ease about its steep, crooked byways, its fine churches, tall old mills and nooks and crannies of eccentric architecture ordered and paid for by centuries of rich clothiers.

Bradford possesses one ancient structure that on its own would make a visit to the town worth while. The curiously narrow small building standing modestly near the parish church did duty for uncounted years as a school and a cottage, until during repairs in the 1850s the then Vicar of Bradford, alerted by the uncovering of a couple of unusually carved stone angels, saw through its disguise. It is just about the finest example of a Saxon church in the country, long since restored to full glory.

By ourselves Jane and I could have spent all afternoon wandering around the town, happening on this and that. But Elizabeth was tugging us away down the riverside path. I held the hand of Mary as she teetered along the top of the river wall with the unfounded confidence of two years old. 'Ah, lickle ducklings,' said Mary, watching six balls of striped fluff paddling in line astern behind their stately mallard mother.

With multiple stops for picking up sticks and swinging on willow trunks, the half-mile from Town Bridge out to Barton Farm on the western outskirts of Bradford lasted a good half-hour. There was a whole sunny afternoon to waste, and we took our time exploring the great fourteenth-century tithe barn, farmhouse and granary at Barton, once the nerve centre of Shaftesbury Abbey's far-flung estates.

Mary went off with Jane to test the echoes in the cavernous barn and see about a brace of ice lollies, while Elizabeth and I sauntered down to the river with our picnic to admire the teenagers happily sneering and flicking their hair on the medieval packhorse bridge. 'I wish *we* had a boat,' Elizabeth murmured dreamily, staring at the water and munching a tomato and marmite sandwich.

Up behind the tithe barn on the Kennet and Avon canal there was no shortage of boats. Narrow boats lay moored among the comfrey and campion at the side of the canal, their sunbathing occupants busy doing nothing over pipes and tea mugs. Supine on the roofs of those boats that were going somewhere, other sun worshippers exchanged chit-chat with Elizabeth as she kept pace with them along the towpath, alternating licks at her ice lolly with puffs at a dandelion clock.

The canal walk is deservedly popular, and the sunshine had brought half Wiltshire out to digest its Sunday lunch by the water, on foot and on bicycles, in pushchairs and wheelchairs. This early in the summer the bank vegetation sprouted uncut, spotted with red and purple flowerheads.

'Mum,' said Elizabeth, 'these nettles don't sting. Why don't they?' Jane showed her the white petals clustered round the stem. 'They're called deadnettles. And that's cow parsley, with the fluffy head.'

'That's Queen Anne's Necklace,' interposed a man as he walked by. 'Leastways that's what we call it hereabouts. Some say wild parsley.' Elizabeth nodded and ran off to watch a brawny chap heaving at a swing bridge to open it for a narrow boat painted with rose-entwined castles.

Mary, meanwhile, had thrown off dress and petticoat, humming tonelessly to herself as she crouched by the side of the towpath squelching clay between her fingers. 'Clay-a, clay-a, muddy-a clay-a' was the burden of her song.

Beyond the swing bridge the troops began to show signs of mutiny. 'I can't walk another step!' declared Elizabeth, sitting down among the deadnettles. 'I want a *dwink*!' Mary backed her up. Things looked sticky for the officers-in-charge until they remembered the emergency rations in the backpack. Apple in one hand and stick in the other, the girls consented to take a short cut with Jane across a meadow to the Avon and a field path back towards Bradford.

I walked on, promising to catch them up. Half a mile more

and one of the Industrial Revolution's most graceful monuments stood ahead, the silvery stone aqueduct built by the eminent engineer John Rennie in the 1790s to carry the canal over the River Avon on its way to Bath. Bowed under its own weight, shaggy with sycamore seedlings and grass tufts clinging to cracks in the stonework, the aqueduct looked down on many-windowed mill buildings by a tumbling weir. In the shadows of one an immense, motionless waterwheel still hung.

In the garden of the Cross Guns pub by the aqueduct, people were still idling over their drinks. Manfully I turned my back on temptation and descended to the riverbank footpath in search of my family.

Soon my shoulders were burdened with a sleepy Mary. Elizabeth would have liked to be up there too, but already Barton Farm's tithe barn was in sight. Could she manage a little bit further, and keep going as far as Town Bridge? With another apple? Yes, she could – just.

If the upper storey of the Bridge Tea Rooms were to lean back only a fraction more, there would be a nasty hole in Bridge Street. The tottery old stone house looks as if a puff of wind would blow it over, but its weight of history and old-fashioned teatime goodies would probably keep it anchored in a hurricane. A beribboned and lace-capped young lady served Coca-cola and chocolate cake to Elizabeth and Mary until they, too, were well and truly ballasted.

FACT FILE

MAP: OS 1:50,000 Landranger Sheet 173 'Swindon and Devizes'

NB 'Town Walk' and 'Country Walk' leaflets with detailed maps available from Bradford-on-Avon Tourist Information Office (see below)

TRAVEL: From west (Bath) – A4, A363. From east (Devizes) – A361 to Trowbridge, A363. From north – M5 to Jct 17, A429 to Chippenham, A350 to Melksham, B3107. From south (Shaftesbury) – A350 to Warminster and Trowbridge, A363. Car park by Town Bridge.

Nearest railway station: Bradford-on-Avon

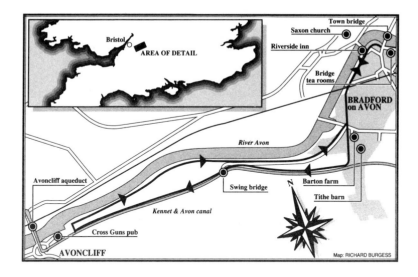

WALK DIRECTIONS: From Town Bridge (826609) follow path by River Avon through Westbury Gardens, past Riverside Inn and on for ½ mile to Barton Farm Country Park. Steps behind tithe barn lead to path (815602) by Kennet & Avon canal. ¾ mile west to Avoncliff aqueduct (804600). Return along path by River Avon.

LENGTH OF WALK: 3 miles – allow 3 hours with young children, including halt at Barton Farm.

CONDITIONS: Well-surfaced pathway, suitable for wheelchairs, pushchairs, bicycles, from Town Bridge to Avoncliff along canal. Return path by river suitable for walking.

GEAR: Ordinary clothes and footwear. Little edible bribes might be useful!

REFRESHMENTS: Bradford-on-Avon: Bridge Tea Shop by Town Bridge; Dandy Lion pub in Market Street welcomes children and offers sticky puddings. Many other pubs and tea shops.
    Barton Farm: tea shop, ices, playground, shops, loos, etc.
    Avoncliff: Cross Guns pub (with garden)

ACCOMMODATION: Swan Hotel, Church Street (0225 868686) and Riverside Inn, 49 St Margaret's Street (0221 63526) both offer family rooms and rates.

FURTHER INFORMATION: Tourist Information Centre, The Library, Bridge Street (0221 65797) – leaflets, guided walks, museum, books

A Voyage with My Father

CERDAGNE RAMBLER, FRENCH PYRENEES

Old man of the mountains: 74-year-old John Somerville

'Snowing,' announced my father, looking out of the Hotel Sun Valley's bedroom window. 'Good thing I packed a vest.'

Booking the 'Cerdagne Rambler' six-day walking holiday with Sherpa Tours, we'd bargained for a few glimpses of snow on far-off mountain peaks. The Cerdagne plateau, after all, lies 6,000 feet up in the French Pyrenees. But the flakes swirling through the streets of Font Romeu this chilly morning looked rather too immediate for comfort. 'Font Romeu is dominated by a vast circle of mountains' promised my father's battered *Guide Bleu* (1919 vintage); but low cloud had blanketed off all views.

In the event, the unseasonably cool weather that had settled over the Cerdagne region turned out to be a blessing in disguise. We covered seven or eight miles a day, in about as many hours, with never a hint of sunburn. Our luggage was carried for us between night stops, freeing our shoulders from the usual strap bruises. For two habitual press-on-regardless walkers it was a salutary change to be wandering in slow motion, with time to enjoy the Cerdagne's delectable landscape.

Perhaps we could have done with a touch more sunshine, but at seventy-four Dad was happy to do without the sweat, flies and sapping heat of a full-blown Mediterranean summer; while for me a feast of spring flowers was still spread unwilted and in full colour across the pastures and through the pine forests of these sheltered uplands.

Within an hour of setting off from Font Romeu we had found our first gentians clustered under the pines, their trumpets closed tight against the melting snow dripping from the branches overhead. I eased one open to see a flash of brilliant royal blue inside. The pines were hung with long green tails of lichen, thriving in the unpolluted air of the mountains: air thin enough at this altitude to make my head spin, as if harbouring a couple of glasses of champagne.

Now the clouds shredded away, revealing the white teeth of the 10,000-foot Carlit Massif mountain range bared at the sky, a stunning first glimpse that distracted us from the task in hand – spotting the waymarks. They were many and confusing: blue flashes, red and white bars, green blobs, pink smears. 'Any waymark's better than none – all roads lead to Rome,' opined Dad, a good practical rule of thumb that served us well through-out the week.

We were climbing steadily into country scored and shaped by Ice Age glaciers. Deep ravines of granite crags enfolded cold, dark lakes (named 'Estany' in Catalan, the local tongue) where taciturn fishermen muttered 'Rien' to my schoolroom 'Avez-vous eu de la chance, monsieur?' Beside Estany de la Pradella we sat on a rock and munched our way through the Hotel Sun Valley's gut-busting picnic, meat from first to last – smoked and unsmoked ham, chicken, pork, sausage.

That night at the Refuge Les Bones Hores ('The Good Time Hangout'?) by the big reservoir of Lac des Bouillouses we fell into good company, a six-strong group of Irish ramblers follow-ing the same circular walk. Other pairs and groups of walkers became familiar figures during the week, seldom seen by day but certain to be encountered swapping yarns over the glasses at each night's hotel. The Irish Rovers (as we christened them) were a mine of information on the flowers, Romanesque churches and wines of the Cerdagne, notable spinners of stories and laughter – 'good crack' merchants, one and all.

How many ramblers with three-quarters of a century under their belts could laugh off a ducking in an icy stream, I wonder? Dad was able to shrug off his tumble into a torrent of meltwater next morning, and dripped dry while I fossicked around with a French language flower book in the wet meadows above Lac des Bouillouses, jewelled with gentians, anemones and star-like white narcissi powdering the grass in drifts like localized snow-falls. Cows and horses cropped the slopes below the snowline, their neck bells donging musically in the clear air.

We spent the afternoon scrambling down a long staircase of tumbled rocks to find Les Angles, a little stone village huddled round its church overlooking the lake, backed by a fearsome metropolis of eccentrically shaped new holiday flats and chalets that covered the hillsides under the ski runs. The Cerdagne is a popular winter sporting area, and some of its villages have lost their souls in the hunt for tourist gold.

But La Llagonne, reached the following afternoon after a day tramping through the forests, was everything Les Angles is no more – tiny, intimate, full of twisting little streets and minia-ture farmyards. In the twelfth-century church St Vincent suf-fered unspeakable tortures in vivid, cruel paintings, and a Catalan Christ stared wide-eyed from His cross.

Now we faced south towards the high white snowfields of the Cambra d'Ase, under whose peaks the tough commandos of the French Army's 1er Regiment de Choc are made even tougher in their training camp in the walled citadel of Mont-Louis. The Cerdagne plateau had been contested for centuries between France and Spain until the Treaty of the Pyrenees in 1659 fixed a border across the mountains and the Cerdagne slipped into French hands. The citadel of Mont-Louis was built in 1679 as a safeguard in case the Treaty fell through, and has lost none of its grimness in the intervening three centuries.

Files of crop-haired soldiers doubled past us under the ramparts, one squat sergeant in a red beret demonstrating on the trot how to kill your man with a blow to the throat. Chilling stuff, but across the valley in the village of Planès we found the Irish Rovers admiring something altogether less menacing – 'La Mezquita', the little mosque, a tiny and beautiful Romanesque church with three apses in clover-leaf shape.

Under the hill slope a few miles along the path lay the hamlet of Mouli del Riu, where at the hotel during a previous holiday Dad had met Pepito the parrot, fluent in both Catalan and French. Alas, said the *patronne*, it was Pepito's day off, but she would convey to him 'l'assurance de nos sentiments les plus distingués'.

M. Corrieu at La Llagonne had stuffed our picnic baguettes with a ham omelette apiece, solid fare that saw us safely into the ski resort of Eyne 2600 (the height of its highest ski run) before rain, chased by snow, closed in. In the morning the snowline had descended not far above the path, and we found the River Ebre too swollen for fording. A tree trunk fallen across the torrent gave us *Boy's Own Paper* visions of a daring scramble across, before realism dictated a more roundabout route to the ancient church and high-piled houses of Llo village, tucked into a crevice of the hills.

In the Hôtel Planes at Saillagouse that night we dined under heads of chamonix and wild boar, while the *patron* entertained a coach party aching for their baked meats with a humorous monologue. Next day was our last; a wood where nightingales fluted breathtakingly, a slippery goat track high in a precipitous gorge and a long climb up to journey's end in Font Romeu.

In the morning Dad and I would drop 6,000 feet to Perpignan and the airport, sole passengers aboard the Cerdagne Canary, the celebrated Train Jaune, winding down the gorges through snaking tunnels and over immense viaducts on one of the world's most scenic railway journeys.

This evening, though, we could take things easy. Before slipping out for a celebratory cognac, I put my head round the bedroom door to see the old man of the mountains already in bed, finishing his whodunit and enjoying a session of almighty yawns. He'd earned them.

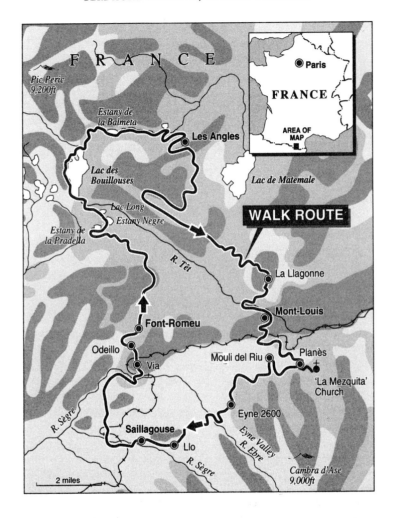

![FACT FILE]

'CERDAGNE RAMBLER' 6-DAY WALKING TOUR: Sherpa Tours, 131a Heston Road, Hounslow, Middlesex TW5 0RD (081 569 4101)

MAPS: Essential to take French IGN 1:25,000 Sheets 2249 ET 'Font Romeu &

Capcir' and 2250 ET 'Bourg-Madame & Mont-Louis' – available from Waterstone's, Stanford's, etc.

ROUTE: 45 mile circular – 6 days

CONDITIONS: Well waymarked; but not for infirm or solo walkers unless very experienced. Working knowledge of map and compass essential. Several descents over broken or rocky ground; some rivers to ford.

GEAR: Full hill-walking gear. Come prepared for both hot and cold weather. Luggage carried by minibus between night stops. Bring mountain flower book, binoculars, camera.

FURTHER READING: *The French Pyrenees* by Neil Lands (Spurbooks)
Michelin Green Guide

Long Trails from the River Bank

FISKERTON TO BURTON JOYCE
RIVER TRENT, NOTTINGHAMSHIRE

Trent anglers wait patiently near Gunthorpe Bridge

A lighting from the little green two-car shuttle train at Fiskerton, on the railway line from Newark to Nottingham, I stopped for a moment to admire the old stationmaster's house beside the track. Tall and ornate, crowned with a forest of chimneys, it spoke of the dignified status of its occupant back in Victorian days before the unmanned Portakabin halt had ever been dreamed of – a splendid gateway, these days, to the rustic pleasures of a ramble along the River Trent.

Down on Fiskerton Wharf the broad, placid Trent slipped gently past, overhung by a crane which once loaded barley malted in the village on to boats making upstream to the breweries of Nottingham. Today the 'princely Trent' carried

139

only a couple of pleasure cruisers, their sailor-capped helmsmen lying back lazily in the cloudy warmth of this muggy summer morning.

The fishermen of Nottingham, however, were out in force, their keep-nets already bulging with roach and bream. Some bareheaded, some in long-peaked baseball caps, they sat at ten-yard intervals all along the river bank, half hidden behind pink clumps of Himalayan balsam, watching their bright orange rod tips as if life itself depended on it. I turned south-west and began to follow the riverside path above their bent backs, serenaded by the 'plop' of lead weights dropping into the dark midriver water.

This section of the Trent Valley, north-east of Nottingham, has two contrasting landscapes separated by the river. To the east flat fields of barley and rough grazing stretched to the skyline, brightened with scarlet poppies, sulphur-yellow rag-wort and white stars of mayweed; while across the river a wooded ridge 150 feet high rose abruptly, shepherding the winding course of the Trent inside the bends of its green rampart.

Down that river cliff opposite Fiskerton Wharf, on 16 June 1487, the terrified supporters of Lambert Simnel, the hapless boy Pretender to the crown, were herded to a fearful slaughter by which Henry VII stamped out the last embers of the Wars of the Roses. So desperate was the bloodshed beside the Trent that day that the track where the massacre of 7,000 rebels took place is still known as the Red Gutter.

Today's scene, however, was entirely peaceful – the silent, intent fishermen, the slow-flowing river sliding by, a gentle breeze rustling the barley under the scarcely moving clouds. I sauntered on, humming to myself and watching a flotilla of great crested grebes ducking and diving along the Trent, until a crashing of water up ahead heralded the thunderous falls of Hazelford weir.

'Here we go,' murmured Jenny Williams the lock keeper, pressing buttons in her little hut to open the lock gates for a pair of sleek launches. 'It's mostly pleasure boats through the lock these days, of course.' She gazed meditatively out of the hut window over the tumbling weir. 'I love this job, but the Trent's not what it was, and not what it could be. They should put more traffic on the river, solve all that crowding and pollution on the roads.'

One hundred and eighty miles long from its source near Stoke-on-Trent to its confluence with the Humber, the River Trent was always a busy waterway. Nowadays the lonely riverside pubs and their jetties, once used by the bargemen and cross-Trent ferry passengers, are packed with anglers and sailors. Some of these inns have done well out of the leisure trade – the old Star and Garter, at the foot of the lane from Bleasby, has swollen and metamorphosed into the bright and bustling Hazelford Ferry Hotel. But the Elm Tree, below Hoveringham a couple of miles upriver, no longer pulls pints; it's been carved up to make three spruce new dwellings.

Shining gin palaces were tied up at the little jetties and slipways next to workaday river boats. *Buccaneer* lay at Hazelford Ferry, long retired from her dashing life as an RAF air–sea rescue launch, grey paint peeling from her superstructure, her streamlined shape still exuding romantic swagger.

'Morning!' smiled the youth in the wheelhouse, rolling a fag. 'Morning!' breezed a man in a red T-shirt, pumping his elbows as he strode past. The anglers were less hearty in their greetings. 'All right?' they muttered, eyes glued to floats. A dredgerman gave me a cheery wave from midstream, where he sat basking on the rail of his blue-painted dredger under a chain of buckets scooping gravel from the bed of the Trent. The buckets clattered tirelessly as water slooshed out of a chute back into the river.

Nearly half a million tons of gravel every year are claimed from the Trent and its surrounding flatlands. Beyond Hazelford Ferry I passed between the river and a great double hollow of disused gravel pit, now flooded and loud with wildfowl cries. A solitary red-sailed dinghy was dipping among its wavelets, under a flight of terns wheeling on slim, crook-elbowed wings.

The sharply metallic, riverine smell of freshly dredged gravel blew across the Trent as I walked on, watching a heron beating ponderously upstream, all but touching his own grey reflection in the river. He settled in the branches of a dead tree, agitating the dozen herons already perched there. They flapped and grumbled, knocking showers of twigs into the water.

A red Land-Rover blocked the path. A young woman with eight rings through her ear and another through her nose was boiling a kettle on a gas stove, surrounded by a silent group of even younger persons. 'British Trust for Conservation Volunteers,' she explained. 'We're digging up the ragwort by hand for the farmer, so he doesn't have to use a spray on it. There are rare flowers in the corner of the field over there.'

'What sort?' I enquired.

'Well—' she grinned sheepishly, 'um . . . I don't exactly know what sort – but I do know they're rare. Have you seen the HALT notices?'

I hadn't, but was soon enlightened. 'Hoveringham Against Local Tip!' shouted the signs from field gates and fence posts. 'Don't let them tip rubbish in our disused gravel pits!' Those big, empty holes in the banks of the Trent would make excellent giant dustbins. But the Trent Valley, peacefully attractive in its own right, has been enriched by the lake-like appearance and wildlife diversity of old pits that have been flooded and managed as recreation assets. An admirable case – so far – of sows' ears into silk purses.

Now the sun slipped through the leaden clouds, and at once the broad face of the river began to sparkle and shimmer. The water bailiff came by, a squat Scot with a squashed conk, fluttering his book of day permits. 'Not fishing?' he challenged me in mock disbelief. 'There's roach, chub, bream – barbel if you can get at them – you're missing out, chum.'

A quick pint of locally brewed bitter in the Unicorn by the three handsome flat arches of Gunthorpe Bridge, and I took to an ancient green lane cutting across a big bend of the Trent. There were wings to my boots – two miles to go, half an hour to beat the train into Burton Joyce station, and a ploughman's lunch calling seductively from the Bromley Arms back on Fiskerton Wharf.

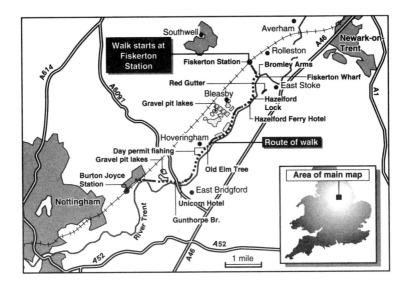

MAPS: OS 1:50,000 Landranger Sheets 120 'Mansfield and The Dukeries'; 129 'Nottingham and Loughborough'

TRAVEL: By road – A1 to Newark-on-Trent; A617 Mansfield road; at Averham, 3 miles west of Newark, turn left on minor road to Rolleston and Fiskerton station.

By rail – From Nottingham or Newark to Fiskerton (train information 0332 32051). *NB Walk takes between 3½ and 4 hours, so allow for this when choosing return train from Burton Joyce to Fiskerton.*

WALK DIRECTIONS: From Fiskerton Station (730520) walk down village street to Fiskerton Wharf and turn right along riverbank path. Route-finding is easy all the way to Burton Joyce station (645433) – just follow the river.

LENGTH OF WALK: 10 miles – allow 4 hours.

CONDITIONS: Grassy riverbank paths – easy underfoot.

GEAR: Walking boots or good shoes are advisable; binoculars for bird life of river and gravel pit lakes.

REFRESHMENTS: Bromley Arms, Fiskerton Wharf (738512); Hazelford Ferry Hotel, Bleasby (725489); Unicorn Hotel, Gunthorpe Bridge (682438) – all on river.

ACCOMMODATION: Hazelford Ferry Hotel (0636 830207); Unicorn Hotel 0602 663612).

FURTHER READING: *Nottinghamshire* by Alan Sillitoe (Grafton)
Bleasby Trail, available Bleasby Post Office

FISHING: Midland Angling Club has stretch of Trent south of Old Elm Tree, Hoveringham. Day permits from bailiff on the spot (£2).

Index